LUPRI STUDIES 2
Editor: Jan Øberg

The Future of the Peace Movements

Katsuya Kodama, Editor
Jan Øberg
Chadwick F. Alger
Radmila Nakarada
Shingo Shibata
Paul Smoker

Lund
University
Press

Lund University Peace Research Institute *LUPRI*
Finngatan 16, S-223 62 Lund, Sweden

The Transnational Foundation for Peace and Future Research *TFF*
Vegagatan 25, S-223 57 Lund, Sweden

Lund University Press
Box 141
S-221 00 Lund, Sweden

© 1989 Authors, Lund University Peace Research Institute *LUPRI* and
The Transnational Foundation for Peace and Future Research *TFF*

Editorial assistant: Ann-Sofi Jakobsson (*LUPRI*)
Language editor on chapter by Kodama: Michael Cheney

Published in Sweden
Studentlitteratur
Lund 1989

Art nr 20153
ISSN 1100 - 5904
ISBN 91-7966-099-1   Lund University Press
ISBN 0-86238-240-8   Chartwell-Bratt Ltd

CONTENTS

Peace Movements and the Future –

An Introduction

Jan Øberg

Lund University Peace Research Institute (LUPRI)
&
The Transnational Foundation for Peace and Future Research
(TFF)

Analysing and understanding peace movements is no easy task. Their goals, value-orientation, forms of organization, social composition, mobilization potential, their societal and political role and their strategies display tremendous variations worldwide.
In most countries media and politicians, and sometimes citizens too, talk about *"the* peace movement" but there is no way in which even those of small nations can all be lumped together.

Most of the chapters in this collection of essays point out the need for more research on social movements in general and peace movements in particular. When approaching the characteristics and functions of peace movements we are, naturally, faced with the matters of definition: Which movements should we study and what is *peace* and what is *a movement?*

Any scholar in the field must also take into account the features of *who, why, how, what, when, by what means etc. of the peace movements themselves as well as of the relations between peace movements and domestic as well as international society.*

In more philosophical terms peace movements, like all other socio-cultural phenomena, can be described as an idea, as organization, as structure and as actors; they are made up of the sum total of *ideas* or visions, of *things and functions* and of individual *human beings*.

And all of them are *expressions of certain cultures or civilizational norms and modes*. Peace activism in the Orient, in Africa and in North America are rather different things and peace work by medical doctors and lawyers differ substantially in terms of goals, methods and expressions from that undertaken by religiously motivated pacifist grassroots such as the Ploughshares or the women in Greenham Common in our own societies.

And they again display a fascinating socio-cultural difference to Buddhist monks or those fighting against nuclear tests in the Pacific or the movements for local self-reliance, justice, cultural identity – and clean water and schooling – among the marginalized and underprivileged, the damned, of the world. There are many worlds and worldviews but only one Earth.

So, there is also the identity-related questions: *Whose* peace? In which *time* – that of the past, the present or the future? Are movements and their mode of operation embodiments of particular messages from the past and are they visionary in the sense that their members are signalling fears and hopes about what is to come?

And, in which *space* do we place them? Some would see them as middle-class, bourgeois or reformist; others would see them as (potentially) revolutionary aiming at grand transformation or striving for socialist values.

Others again would see them as "combi-movements" gathering a wide variety of green, women's, ecological, spiritual sentiments and political – or anti-political in a György Konradian sense – undercurrents which, to a certain degree, link up with the struggle of the underprivileged, exploited of the underdeveloped societies of world community. That is, as a major global movement for a third way opposing the Euro-centric "solutions" of capitalism and socialism and aiming at development, peace and social change from below. In each there is a truth. In none of them we find the whole truth. In some of these visualizations we find a mix of empirical evidence and hopes and aspirations. Few phenomena have invited so much discussion as who the (real) peace movements are, what peace movements "should" do or what the true type of peace worth struggling for is. Sadly enough, it can be asserted that many of the movement people themselves have devoted a remarkable amount of energy on fighting each other rather than those whom they consider their "enemy".

Be this as it may, the emerging field of peace movement research is an intellectually fascinating and politically important one. As some of the authors in this volume emphasize it *forces us to rethink many sociological categories and concepts.*

The *"rise and fall" of peace movements* in different times and socio-political spaces gives rise for many an interested scholar-cum-citizen to ponder essential issues what is the nature of democracy and participation? What are the relations between freedom, human rights, and peace in modern industrial society and in the world system? What is the interplay between local-global development and peace? How do different social settings and historical circumstances influence the collective choice of strategy within a movement? What can we learn about mobilization for social change from the study of peace movements?

And, not the least, what is the structure and function of individual and social energies devoted to work for peace – what makes citizens struggle for what issues and for how long; what makes them end their work, choose something else or give up? Is it true that activists are operating much more on fear than on hopes, that a Cold War and militarization creates movements whereas détente and disarmament – even the present tendency to stop the Cold War – causes movements to fall. And how are movements financed, where and when are they vulnerable, when have they accomplished their mission? Indeed, how is citizenry consciousness raised and who makes history?

A "grand" theory – or a cluster of theories – which holds the potential to explain all this in a manner satisfactory to scholars, citizens and movement actors alike will hardly ever be found. The diversity and complexity of the real world is too great for that.

The question must also be raised whether research on peace movements in general and this particular search for a "grand theory" is intended to serve the discipline of sociology, the movements themselves, the goal of peace, or the social engineering and manipulations by repressive or authoritarian regimes and even some mainstream democracies whose leaderships dislike peace movements?

We have not even caught a fraction of the global picture. Since this volume focus mainly on various aspects of peace movements in the overdeveloped world and present authors and problems from Eastern Europe, Sweden, Japan, Great Britain, and the United States it is pertinent to recognize our own limitations.

If the struggle for peace gave priority to saving human lives in a maldeveloped world in which 60,000 dies every day unnecessarily, peace movements would become development movements. For the underprivileged two thirds of humankind, peace means shelter, food, medicine, clean water, literacy, roads, and social care at just a minimum level. They die in structural, system-based violence, not in wars. Modern warfare, particularly nuclear weaponry, have killed far fewer fellow human beings than the Western-generated maldevelopment of global society, actually "only" some 2-3000 per day since 1945.

If this gross civilian violence were the first object of peace activism and *if* the misery of the underprivileged millions were conceptualized as causally linked to the overdevelopment and affluence, to the outrageously extravagant life styles that we take for granted in our societies *then* the peace movements would basically be working for and practise new globally acceptable life styles in the North-Western hemisphere, they would be conscious consumer movements and challenge conventional economics and their members would operate on a kind of global ethics the basical norms of which would be something like: "Act in such a manner that permanence and diversity of the biosphere is never impaired and act so that no harm would be caused to others if everybody else did what you do!"

The peace movement problems discussed in this volume would, by and large, be considered a luxury by the majority of peoples worldwide. They would hardly understand why, in the 1980s, peace movements in Eastern and Western Europe devoted so much energy on quarrelling about whether peace or freedom comes first. If they knew about it they would probably ask how we could spend so much intellectual and emotional capital on discussing which weapons in the United States or Europe to protest against first or how movements could spend their time accusing each other of being allies of this or that super power?

If asked, the damned of the world system would probably answer that the following statement by Mahatma Gandhi describes eloquently what they see as urgent task to be undertaken *also* by us in the overdeveloped nations :

"I will give you a talisman. Whenever you are in doubt
or when the self becomes too much with you, apply the following test:
Recall the face of the poorest and the weakest man
whom you may have seen and ask yourself
if the step you contemplate is going to be of any use to him.
Will he gain anything by it?
Will it restore him to a control over his own life and destiny?
In other words, will it lead to Swaraj for the hungry and spiritually starving
millions?
Then you will find your doubts and your self melting away."

No one is to be blamed. We are here facing one of the most essential paradoxes of our time and an unavoidable one at that: Whatever we do for peace will be limited in scope. It is a citizen's duty to address the problems of his or her own country, i.e. of the few. In doing so, there is a risk that we implicitly ignore the needs of the many.

Active peace movement people are still a small minority. They can act in accordance with their own limited needs or that of their local, national or regional society *as they see these – collective – needs.* They act on behalf of someone else – fellow citizens, unborn generations, the right to live without fear of nuclear extinction or for freedom and civil liberties.

The interesting question is: How far does this action on behalf of someone else reach? How far beyond one's own society *can* it reach and with what implications? All movements carry a nucleus of visionary individuals or smaller groups who want to spread a message. How to balance between single issues, the specific goals for the few and the general transformative messages to the many that *must* be reached to bring global change? We must begin with ourselves and our own problems, say some. We must have a programme and a plan of action and convince others, say others.

In all work for social change and peace there is an element of *elitism* and of *appeal*, of a self-imposed responsibility or representativity on behalf of the many.

We will seek in vain for a unifying peace model and I think it is an illusion to hope for all types of peace movements joining in the realization of a single peace goal such as nuclear disarmament, the UN, world government, global meditation, just socio-economic development etc. Peace must embody the struggle for unity in diversity, indeed peace implies diversity – i.e. co-existence between many and probably very different "peaces" around the globe.

Therefore, understanding the *compatibility between* different peace concepts, policies and movement strategies worldwide – the knitting together of a gigantic patchwork of peace activities forming "world peace(s)" – is an urgent scholarly, cultural and political task.

How can the most effective and fruitful peace thoughts, goals and visions be combined, re-enforce each other or at least not damage it other, how can we learn from each other and form networks and transnational links on the way to a just, ecological balanced, ethically and spiritually informed and materially acceptable (not too high, not too low) standards which, in sum, qualifies to be called humane while preserving the diversity of the biosphere of which we are all an integrated part?

Second, it seems to me that the *existential* dimension must be addressed. As we have stated above, much peace movement activity consist in appealing and convincing others. It is natural since the activist has come to some clarity or sensed an urgency that he or she want others to pay attention to. We must do something about this! – the activist says.

This appeal for change is legitimate and necessary. But the outward, externally directed activity of appealing to others sometimes stands in the way for changing one's own ways of thinking and acting. Inner change remains untouched.

Governments are by definition actors which find security and peace through identifying the threat, i.e. the root cause of the evil, as "the Other" and seeking peace (disarmament, arms control, non-proliferation etc.) through the appeal to other governments. "Please take the first step, then we shall follow" or "When they have agreed with us and met our priority requirements, we may reduce our own arsenals". The Soviet Union under Mikhail Gorbachev is an impressive exception to this vicious argument these years, but this is the general norm in the international community. Few, it would seem, are aware of its collective effects: if everybody demands that *others* take the first step before they do, nothing will ever happen.

So too with movements. The single activist may be marching the streets, but there is little in the movement's organization, decision-making processes, its language, its pattern of social intra-action and inter-action with society at large that *embodies* change itself or signifies that the movement as a social actors can be seen as the *seed* of a new society, a vision or of peace.

Movement people *work* for peace, they don't *exist* for peace – which would, admittedly, be a tall order. Most Western movements have planned demonstrations with a view to questions such as "By which slogans can we get most people to gather at the central square of our town?" Gandhi who embodied an existence *for* and *in* peace would not have asked such a question, he would say: What is the correct thing to do in this situation, if even one does it that is important. If I can do it others can – and then he would start marching or practicing non-violent actions and, in the best of cases, others would mobilize.

This is where the argument between "realists" and "idealists" within the movements often appears. Appealing for single issues and influencing the political decision-making bodies in order to achieve some "real" political results within a shorter time span is often preferred to changing life styles, thinking and acting according to a lifelong struggle etc.

The *result* is put before the *process*. One may say that this, again, is quite far from the way we might think that Gandhi would have approached the problems. He would have quoted himself that goals and means are inseparable.

However, it is another unavoidable paradox that we shall all have to live by. The two ways of grappling with peace and social change are legitimate and not necessarily incompatible. However, there remains – again – the question of how to hit the right balance and, deeper, is such a balance ever to be found. Isn't it all a permanent experiment with empathy, new ways of thinking, acting and civil courage?

Perhaps the most important function of peace movements is to be a guardian of government policies in this – particular – sense: Any state or government has amassed extreme power over the citizenry of their own society and some over virtually all others too. The states could do things that would cause irreparable damage locally as well as globally.

Some power or force must be invested with and possessed by those who are not part of that state or government power for the simple reason that it could do wrong. One of Gandhi's most important messages is, I think, that he advocated non-violence because it can never cause irreparable damage. The gun can. Non-violence permits me to say: I am sorry, I was wrong. The actor who is omnipotent and commands the power to kill will be much more inclined to maintain that "might makes right" and that the hurting, harming, killing and lying was justified. Violence binds the subject to the deed. The non-violent fighter can admit that he or she was wrong because the effects of the deed is not irreversible.

Most governments around the world can act and do act in ways that cause irreversible damage every day. Social movements don't. Both can be wrong, movements can admit it, governments generally can't. This is why social movements are dearly needed in any political system and any culture and this is also the explanation why they are – and should be – considered a challenge to the state and its increasingly omnipotent powers: *they can provide a social space for humility, repentance, care, consolation, wisdom and creativity and, not the least, individual responsibility – asking not only about human rights but also about human duties and obligations locally and globally – that no other social institution in the modern Western culture seems to provide today.*

Social movements are such soft things that deep changes are made of but only in the very long run. There are no short cuts to peace – as we are reminded by Lao Tze in *"Tao Teh King"* (6th century B.C.):

> *"The softest thing in the world*
> *dashes against and overcomes the hardest;*
> *that which has no (substantial) existence enters*
> *where there is no crevice.*
> *I know hereby what advantage belongs*
> *to doing nothing (with a purpose)."*

Finally a few words about this volume.

Chadwick Alger discusses the wide variety of social movements in different socio-economic settings and places peace movements in the context of wider transformation in the global system, in what he calls the larger constellation of organizations working for human betterment.

Like several others, Alger is interested in finding out how "peace" relates to, or overlaps with, development, human rights, ecological balance, social justice etc. Do movements with these different foci all confront the same "common foe"? Is there a general social cosmology, a notion of a dominant social paradigm that underlies all these problem areas as a dominant, programmed civilizational "way of thinking" which can be seen as the common foe?

In tracing the changes in the conceptualization he, as many other thinkers on peace and movement and research, considers that over time peace has increasingly come to mean "an unfolding potential that grows out of the pursuit of peace. Says Alger, "the broader definition of peace reveals a diversity of human activities through which peace can be pursued, implying that all occupations have peacemaking potential. Only now is this potential beginning to be discovered".

Perhaps, he says, what all social movements have in common is that they converge on the idea of life itself, against the colonization of the life-world. They rise because the minimal standards of "the good life" are increasingly threatened by modern technological developments. Intuitive awareness of problems and consequences for the global human system and the biosphere is what motivates individuals, combined with some loose vision of desirable worlds ahead. In this sense movements become more and more important and gather strength as catalysts of hitherto ignored opportunities.

In principle, Alger argues with support from Third World thinkers such as Rajni Kothari, there is no reason why Third World movements against poverty, peace movements beginning with anti-militarism and pacifism, women's movement struggling for justice and ecological movements for sustainable development should not converge and serve as force multipliers for each other. They are addressing different aspects of the same civilizational malaise. In one word, social movements embody a new holistic analysis and vision and they help us imagine a new kind of transnational politics.

Thus, local communities assert themselves in new ways when, together with each other and the social movements and world NGOs, they confront the consequences of macro-structures and decide to opt out of that game and re-unite in a new one. The experience no longer comes from governments or the experts, it comes from a revitalized employment of all capacities and faculties of ordinary fellow citizens who in direct and indirect ways network and support each other in what is virtually the same struggle against a common foe.

To succeed and grow further, visions are needed, not just despair, anxiety or anger. There must also be hope and love, human compassion as a fuel for activism. Therefore, the study of local responses worldwide to macro intrusion in the life-world of people is a crucial research priority. Why should municipalities not, sooner or later, engage in foreign policy and global affairs in transnational manner, Alger asks?

Radmila Nakarada deals with peace movements and peace thinking in Eastern Europe. Hers is a broad approach seeking the "missing links between general civilizational formulas and their concrete implementation" in a regional historical reality.

Her focus is on the relations between peace and democracy and freedom and she traces the development of peace conceptualization in the collective consciousness through various stages, through a) reticence about peace, b) democratic peace and c) the widening scope of the social change agents in the light of the newly created social space provided by the reforms in the Soviet Union and its relations with Eastern Europe.

Peace in this regional setting, she maintains, must be understood as internal; reformists will increasingly recognize that there are limits to what can enthusiastically be imported from the West – such as marketization. The two grand projects of European origin, socialism and capitalism, Marxism and liberalism – are in crisis and have caused civilizational troubles. The link between inner reforms and the development of a trustworthy internal actor is established convincingly. We are again at the crossroads of balancing as I have pointed out above. Domestic changes for peace and freedom can only turn its back to the global problematique in limited periods; society cannot be changed at home without being infused with the norms and demands of a more just world order.

It is fascinating how East German movements have understood this much better than those of the West who seldom, in their work for peace, challenge civilian society, consumerism, global maldevelopment or the de facto limitation of democracy that we can identify also in liberal, parliamentary democracies and in their operation in other parts of the world.

At the same time, Nakarada points out, Eastern European peace movements are not sufficiently critical of the Western establishment and they are – understandably one may say at this junction – too Eurocentric to grasp the global peace and development problematique. Like they consider some of the Western movements "luxurious" in their choice of certain foci, Third World movements would find Eastern European ones even more Eurocentric than the Western movements – and both quite incapable of understanding the peace problems and concepts of other cultures.

Shingo Shibata addresses the sociological implications of the bombings of Hiroshima and Nagasaki or what he calls "sociocide" and others have called "omnicide". The study of the lives of the survivors, hibakushas, is the focal point of our contemporary understanding of what exterminism implies. They provide an entirely new task for social and humanistic sciences and, he maintains, essentially we are all hibakushas in that we as world citizens are either atomic bombs victims, radiation victims, constantly threatened by nuclearism or victims of the particular nuclear blackmail that is embedded in the deterrence system on which life on Earth hinges.

Shibata then traces the "rise and fall" of peace movements in Japan. It – or they, rather – are not economically motivated, they do not represent single interests, their aim is to help further a new way of thinking (in an Einsteinian sense), they are necessarily inter- or transnational, historic and future-oriented and come in countless shapes. This is how they are different and challenge the sociological investigator.

Finally, Shibata offers a case study and describes a successful signature campaign independently initiated and organized by the Gensuikyo movement in 1985-86. Among other aspects, Shibata analyses the organizational and mobilization dynamics and ends up offering us some elements towards the construction of a theory of social movements. The important conclusion is that "the developmental process of groups is at the same time the process of development of individual personalities that make up the groups". Personal development, he implies, goes hand in hand – in the successful movement – with common interests and harmonization in a societal process of mutual education and dialogue.

Katsuya Kodama presents some of the findings from his pioneering survey-based analysis of selected Swedish movements which will later be published as his dissertation. Kodama's focus here is on who are the peace "new" movements and how do they think in comparison with the general public? He describes the Christian Peace movement, the Peace Committee, the Swedish Peace and Arbitration Society, Women's International League for Peace and Freedom, Women for Peace. He examines their educational and occupational background and finds, with reference to social movement theory, that peace activists to a higher degree than the general public hold post-material values, that they share a strong anti-nuclear and pacifist ideology which aims to transcend the European bloc system, that they assign almost equal responsibility on the United States and the Soviet Union for the arms race and that peace activists are generally more environmentalist and feminist-oriented than the general public.

Kodama draws the important conclusion that "peace movements challenge not only a government's policy on military issues but also call into question social structures, ways of thinking, life styles, etc. The society they are pursuing might be called the post-materialist society, civil society, green society, post-industrial society, alternative society or feminist society. ...peace movements challenge the present male-authoritarian militaristic society and attempt to transform it into a society in which equality, environmentalism, solidarity, self-determination and peace are the basic principles. The extent to which such a society has been realized is, in my view, one of the most important indicators of success or failure of peace movement".

Paul Smoker's article introduces the idea of action-research into this field. He describes how the Richardson Institute for Peace Studies at Lancaster University helped the Campaign for Nuclear Disarmament (CND) in Barrow in Furness undertake an opinion survey in 1985, how the movement made up a strategy for influencing public opinion in the light of the survey analysis and how the results of the campaign were measured in a follow up survey a year later. The case deals with the procurement and production by Great Britain of Trident submarines begun in the early 1980s at the Vickers submarine complex in Barrow. The surveys examined the knowledge and attitudes of a representative sample of citizens concerning the submarine project. It is an interesting illustration of the problems of local communities which are strongly dependent on military production and it is probably unique in the sense that it shows how scholars can make a contribution to activism.

Smoker and his team identified that there was a group of 9% of the sample who thought Trident was necessary for the defence of the country but who did *not* think the expenditure on Trident submarines was justified. This group became the target group of the campaign. CND decided to produce a campaign material that stressed the costs of the Tridents (and emphasizing that 50% of it was to be spent in the United States) as well as the local possibilities for alternative production that would make the future of Vickers more secure.

The follow up survey reveals that the campaign was quite effective and did have an impact on the knowledge and attitudes of citizens in Barrow. However, other events during the year probably also played a role. So, science does not have to be only in the service of the military. Social movements can benefit from professional assistance – and social science gains new insights when it has such access to "experiments" in the real world.

Finally, the volume contains a bibliography including books, articles and book chapters of peace movement research compiled by Kodamasan. We hope this will be useful for further readings and studies in the field.

Regrettably, this is the last publication from the Lund University Peace Research Institute (LUPRI) which has accumulated a peace research competence and poured out some 15,000 pages of scientific publications since 1963. Thanks not the least to Katsuya Kodama, one of LUPRI's main priorities has been peace movement research and we are happy that this particular publication rounds off these productive years.

We publish it in co-operation with the Transnational Foundation for Peace and Future Research (TFF), an independent, not-for-profit research foundation, also in Lund, which was established in 1986 and marks the transition of forms but not of our commitment to doing peace research for a more humane future.

We believe that peace research and equally important future-oriented scholarly disciplines will always survive, like the water drop on the stone, by "softer" and subtler developments into the crevices of modern society. Like movements, like concerned citizens, the all seed of new thinking. Sometimes, we have to admit, the stones of large bureaucracies such as (some) universities are so hard and perhaps have no crevices to enter into even over long time. They become stumbling blocks, embodying self-sufficient worldviews and intellectual closedness.

Then we happily find new ways of thinking, new forms of organization, new growth materials and new seeds elsewhere. Like the movements struggling for a more humane world in the larger perspective. Maybe, in the long run, that is – simply – what change is all about?

Creating Global Visions for

Peace Movements

Chadwick F. Alger
Mershon Center
The Ohio State University

Peace movements are in a state of flux that is on the one hand presenting new opportunities for increased grassroots participation and impact, but on the other hand creating difficulties in the self-identity of these groups and of individuals affiliated with them. Many participants in peace movements thought that they understood with certainty the meaning of peace only to be perplexed by debate about positive peace versus negative peace and direct violence versus structural violence.

They are challenged and encouraged by increasing emphasis on the significance of grassroots initiatives; but at times they are puzzled by simultaneous emphasis on the importance of transnational movements. They saw distinctions between peace movements and movements focused on other issues such as development, human rights and ecology; but increasingly they hear those involved in these movements declare that they too are workers for peace – as when the Pope declared: "Development is another word for peace." What should be the self-identity of groups and individuals working for peace? What should be their global vision of a movement toward peace in which they fit their own efforts?

There are those who perceive the growing "lack of focus" of "the peace movement" as a sign of weakness; but it may also be interpreted as a sign of intellectual vitality, of openness to broader visions and new ideas, and as a sign of willingness to acknowledge the reality of growing interconnections between scattered arenas of peacelessness that were once perceived to be separate and independent of each other.

We tend to accept this latter view, sensing that the present state of flux is provoking a global dialogue of contending and complementary views out of which will emerge new visions of peace potential from a global perspective. It is the purpose of this paper to pose some of the difficult challenges, and opportunities, that the present state of flux now offers to those endeavoring to understand where their particular peace efforts fit into the global peace movement.

Where does the peace movement fit in the larger constellation of organizations working for human betterment? It will be useful at the onset to pose the question in terms of three clearly differentiated possibilities. First, does the broadening definition of peace that is emerging out of global practice and dialogue suggest that peace is *the* goal toward which humanity is striving? This approach would say that the pursuit of nonviolence, economic justice, human rights and ecological balance would be best perceived as facets of the struggles for peace.

Second, is peace *one* of the prime goals for achieving human betterment, along with economic justice, human rights and ecological balance? From this perspective, peace overlaps with each of the other goals, producing the need for coordination, but each goal is seen to require its own distinctive movement. Third, do the separate struggles for peace, economic justice, human rights and ecological balance suggest that all confront a common foe, such as Milbrath's notion of a Dominant Social Paradigm. (Milbrath, 1988) Does contemporary experience point toward the need for an integrated assault on this common foe that could require reconceptualization, and reorganization, of the array of social movements that arose before it was realized that all were facing a common foe?

1 Three transformations in peace thinking

A fundamental factor in the challenges now confronted by peace movements is the global dialectic in peace thinking in the Twentieth Century that has produced three fundamental transformations. The first transformation was from a definition of peace limited to 'stopping the violence' to a much broader notion of peace as reflected in the UN Declaration of the Preparation of Societies for Life in Peace. This definition has been aptly summarized by the United Nation University as:

> The removal of institutional obstacles and the promotion of structural conditions facilitating the growth of socio-cultural, economic and political trends, aiming at and leading to Life in Peace understood as both subjective life styles and objective living conditions congruent with basic peace values such as security, non-violence, identity, equity and well-being as opposed to insecurity, violence, alienation, inequity and deprivation. (United Nations University, 1986)

This broader definition of peace has emerged out of a great global dialogue – in the UN system, non-governmental organizations, and scholarly debate – that has demonstrated that people in different circumstances experience peacelessness as a result of a variety of conditions, such as sickness, poverty, oppression, war or threat of war, threat to cultural survival, and pollution of water, air and food. This great global dialogue suggests that progress toward peace from a global perspective requires overcoming simultaneously a diversity of causes of peacelessness. This is partly necessary because there are causal connections between war, injustice, oppression and pollution. But equally important is the fact that peace strategies can only gain global acceptance if they simultaneously attempt to overcome the primary causes of peacelessness worldwide.

The second transformation in peace thinking is closely intertwined with the first. The broadening definition of peace now makes it increasingly apparent that peace is not a condition that a few leaders alone can attain for the people of the world. As long as peace was believed to be attainable 'simply' by stopping aggression and violence (i.e. negative peace), it was plausible, although I believe this too was an illusion, that a few leaders could secure peace for the masses. But the broadened notion of peace (including also positive peace) clearly reveals that a diversity of sectors of any society, and a diversity of sectors of relationships between societies, contribute to peacelessness and thus must be involved in peacemaking. This does not mean that governmental leaders, and a variety of non-governmental institutions and leaders, no longer have important roles to play in peacebuilding. But it does mean that they cannot attain a strong and lasting peace alone without widespread knowledge, participation and support from the people of the world.

A third transformation in peace thinking largely follows from the first two and is perhaps still more implicit than explicit. This transformation sees peace as an unfolding potential that grows out of the pursuit of peace. This suggests that the further we move toward the attainment of our present notion of peace the more highly developed will our future image of peace and the possibility of achieving this new image. This is dramatically different from the perspective that looks on peace as a return to conditions before war broke out, or that looks upon peace as a resolution or settlement or certain conflicts so that people can return to other pursuits, assured that the settlement will guarantee the peace. Instead, the broader definition of peace reveals a diversity of human activities through which peace can be pursued, implying that all occupations have peacemaking potential. Only now is this potential beginning to be discovered.

Naturally, there are those who feel uncomfortable with this multifaceted transformation in peace thinking. They still cling to the notion that "stopping the violence" or "banning the bomb" must be achieved first, as a prerequisite for achieving other goals which they prefer to refer to by terms such as social justice, economic well-being and ecological balance. This is not surprising because there is indeed much violence in the world, and fear of widespread destruction by nuclear weapons – even destruction of the planet's ecosystem – is a conscious concern of people all over the world. Efforts to limit, and even abolish, the production and deployment of these weapons must be intensified. But for millions of people, other forms of peacelessness – malnutrition, disease, poverty, racial discrimination, sexual discrimination, and destruction of culture – are even more tangible parts of everyday life. It would seem obvious that a sound foundation for worldwide peace can be constructed only by simultaneous responsiveness to pleas for relief from people whose lives are made miserable by a diversity of causes of peacelessness.

This broad approach is supported by experience in humankind's great peace laboratories, the League of Nations and the United Nations system. When viewed from a seventy year perspective, these laboratories have demonstrated that so-called negative peace strategies (stopping the violence) such as collective security, peaceful settlement, peacekeeping and disarmament have repeatedly had very limited success. Workers in both the League and the UN laboratory have found it necessary to broaden the agenda to include other causes of peacelessness. Thus we see a dramatic long-term growth in concern for economic well-being, self-determination, and human rights, and more recently, attention to ecological issues. Some have mistakenly concluded that these global organizations, failing to keep the peace, decided instead to deal with more tractable issues in a strategy of avoidance. Instead, I believe that feedback from these laboratories has demonstrated that the agenda had to be broadened because negative peace strategies cannot be successful without simultaneously achieving a certain degree of success on positive peace issues. At the same time it has been learned that positive peace strategies may at times be more effective and make the need for using negative peace strategies unnecessary. (This section was extracted from Alger, 1987.)

2 The "common foe" approach to contemporary social movements

A number of scholars perceive an array of social movements, including the peace movement, to be struggling against a common foe. Milbrath sees close linkage between "the struggle for peace, the struggle for partnership between the sexes and the struggle for protection of the integrity of the environment". He notes that all three problems "have their roots in the same social malady – the Dominant Social Paradigm (DSP) that dominates modern Western thinking". The DSP has the following belief elements:
1. Human should dominate nature.
2. It is natural for men to dominate women.
3. Power is the key to control and security.

4. Economic strength, science, and technology should be stressed in order to increase power.
5. Competition, and markets, should be stressed in order to maximize achievement and power.
6. We must take large risks in order to maximize achievement and power.
7. We do not need government foresight and planning; the market will take care of the future.
8. There are no limits to growth.
9. Human progress (in the sense of DSP) need never cease.

Milbrath sees a deeper belief hidden behind the nine listed: "Most 'other' creatures, human and non-human, are our competitors and/or enemies – they must be dominated and controlled in order for us to feel secure." (Milbrath, 1988, 16) He believes that we must recognize "the common roots" of environmental, feminist and peace problems and create a "new belief paradigm that will enable humans to live harmoniously with each other and with all the other creatures in nature". (Milbrath, 1988)

Other scholars are reaching strikingly similar conclusions. John J. De Deken, in a study of the current peace movement in Flanders, asserts that the "new" social movements such as the green movement and the peace movement "try to defend the integrity of the life-world as such, against the one-sided process of purposive-oriented rationalization. In a way they form an oppositional power against the *colonization* of the life-world". (De Deken, 1988, 5-6) Karl Werner Brand claims that the peace movement is only the top of an iceberg of the post-materialistic, anti-technocratic opposition. (Brand 1983,214; cited by De Deken, 1988, 8-9.) Claus Offe has observed that contemporary social movements

> converge on the ideal that life itself – and the minimal standards of 'good life' as defined and sanctioned by modern values – is threatened by the bland dynamic of military, economic, technological and political rationalization; and that there are no sufficient and sufficiently reliable barriers within dominant political and economic institutions that could prevent them from passing the threshold to disaster. (Offe, 1985, 853; cited by Mendlovitz and Walker, 1987, 10.)

Brian Tokar's study of *The Green Alternative* has a quite similar ring when he notes that the "Greens are not a single issue movement...As ecology describes the interconnections among all living things, an ecological politics need to embrace the interconnectedness of all aspects of our social and political lives and institutions...The Domination of human by human is an ecological problem". (Tokar, 1987, 55-56) He lists the "four pillars" of the West German Greens: ecology, social justice and responsibility, democracy in politics and in the economy and nonviolence. This treatise on the Greens takes up the "four pillars" in this order, progressing from ecology to nonviolence, and concluding that "war has always been an ecological problem". (124) (In contrast, Western peace movements would tend to begin with nonviolence, perhaps moving on to economic well-being, then social justice, and ending with ecology.)

Rajni Kothari too perceives the emergence of an array of social movements responsive to a common foe. He observes that "an unprecedented convergence is taking place between the environment and feminist movements, between these two and the human rights movement (the latter is becoming wholly redefined), and between all of them and the peace movement". (Kothari, 1987, 401) Kothari describes Indian movements that have arisen in opposition to the "development-strategies of the state". He observes that the state is now perceived as an agent of technological modernization, with a view more to catching up with the developed world and emerging on the world and regional scenes as a strong state (hence the vast sums spent on armaments) than coping with the pressing, often desperate, needs and demands of the poor. (Kothari, 1984, 544) He perceives tendencies

> that seek, on the one hand, to integrate the organized economy into the world market and, on the other hand, remove millions of people from the economy by throwing them in the dustbin of history – impoverished, destitute, drained of their own resources and deprived of minimum requirements of health and nutrition, denied 'entitlement' to food and water and shelter – in short, an unwanted and dispensable lot whose fate seems to be 'doomed'.

Kothari sees "grass-roots movements and non-party formations" as springing "from a deep stirring of consciousness and an intuitive awareness of a crisis that could conceivably be turned into a catalyst of new opportunities". These new movements are attempting to "open alternative political spaces" outside the traditional arenas of party and government. (Kothari, 1983, 598)

Kothari observes that the very content of politics has been redefined. Issues that "were not so far seen as amenable to political action...now fall within the purview of political struggle". (Kothari, 1984, 552) These include people's health, rights over forests and other community resources, and women's rights. Not limited to economic and political demands, the struggle extends to ecological, cultural and educational issues. Examples include people's movements to prevent the felling of trees on the foothills of the Himalayas, the miners' struggle in Chattisgarh (a predominantly tribal belt in Madhya Pradesh), and organization of landless activists in Andhra Pradesh, a peasant's organization in Kanakpura in Karnataka against the mining and export of granite, and a movement for regional autonomy in the tribal belt of Bihar and Orissa. While basing his analysis on Indian experience, Kothari sees these movements as part of a "phenomenon [that] has more general relevance". (Kothari, 1984, 560) They are, in his view, responsive to

> a new...phase in the structure of world dominance, a change
> of the role of the state in national and subnational settings, and
> a drastically altered relationship between the people and what
> we (half in jest and half in deception) call 'development'.
> (Kothari, 1983, 613)

It is obvious that the Greens, and those opposing the "colonization" of the life-world, "the one-sided process of purposive-oriented rationalization", the Dominant Social Paradigm, and "the structure of world dominance" share some goals with all peace movements. But Europeans cited tend to commence their analysis with ecology and Third World scholars tend to use poverty as the point of origin. On the other hand, peace paradigms, and peace movements, tend to begin with nonviolence, with poverty coming next and ecology last. How should the increase in overlapping agendas of peace, ecological and anti-poverty movements be taken into account? 1) Should the peace movement insist that overcoming violence, poverty and destruction of the environment – and other peace issues – all be treated as part of an expanding peace movement? 2) Should these various movements maintain their separate identities while cooperating on common agenda items? 3) Should a new generation of movements be developed that provide an integrated strategy against an increasingly visible common foe?

Kothari does not answer these difficult questions but gropes toward one in pointing out that "the important point is...the interrelationship of dimensions and movements, of a holistic approach to life, which goes against the grain of modern scientific culture and its emphasis on specialization and fragmentation". (Kothari, 1987, 401) He has a vision in which

> as the feminist values become more generalized, a holistic approach will develop. It will be an approach that is also plural and based on complementarities. This is more likely to happen in the non-Western world than in the West because of the former's traditions of plurality and androgny. (Kothari, 1987, 401)

3 Social movements in global perspective

There is a growing literature illuminating the dynamic response by social movements in all parts of the world to a pressing array of social problems. If these movements are to cope with powerful transnational production, marketing, communications and military organizations that are intruding on local space, they will require, at the very least, some kind of shared global vision of their common enterprise. Kothari says: "The basic question is: can this activism, all these 'movements' produce a macro challenge, a general transformation (whether one calls it a revolution or not)?" (Kothari, 1987, 401)

Writing out of experience with the Lokayan movement in India, D. L. Sheth perceives a new mode of politics arising across regional, linguistic, cultural and national boundaries. It encompasses peace and anti-nuclear movements, environmental movements, women's movements, movements for self-determination of cultural groups, minorities and tribes, and a movement championing non-Western culture, techno-sciences and languages. Importantly, this new politics is "not constricted by the narrow logic of capturing state power". Rather Sheth discerns the need for new insights on micro-macro linkage. He concludes:

It is the dialectic between micro-practice and macro-thinking that will actualize a new politics of the future...In brief, a macro-vision is the prime need of these groups and movements, and this can be satisfied only by a growing partnership between activists and intellectuals in the process of social transformation. (Sheth, 1983, 23)

Sheth notes that one of the three principles on which a "new politics" is based is "an awareness that the local power structures against which (local) people are fighting derive their power from macro structures of the present national and international order". (Sheth, 1983, 7) In response, he notes that "a macro theory of transformative political action is required which is based on the values and practice of democracy and which has synthesizing potentials for integrating the perspectives and actions of various issue-based movements in a larger framework of transformation". (Kothari, 1987, 249) But Sheth insists that "it is necessary that a theory of alternative action emerge through the process of grassroots movements making their impact on the global thinking, rather than the other way round". (Sheth, 1987, 246)

Swedish peace researchers Mats Friberg and Björn Hettne describes a challenging vision of an emerging worldwide "Green" movement that offers an alternative to the "Blue" (market, liberal, capitalist) and the "Red" (state, socialism, planning). They reject "mainstream development thinking" in which "the state is always seen as the social subject of the development process". Instead, from the Green perspective, they see that "the human being or small communities of human beings are the ultimate actors. The state can at most be an instrument for this ultimate actor". (Friberg and Hettne, 1982, 23) In other words, Friberg and Hettne consider that "the tribes and nations of the world are much more basic units of development" than states. They use human needs as a starting point from which the following are derived:

Cultural identity – the social unit of development is a culturally defined community and the development of this community is rooted in the specific values and institutions of this culture.
Self-reliance – each community relies primarily on its own strength and resources.
Social justice – development programs should give priority to those most in need.

Ecological balance – the resources of the biosphere are utilized in full awareness of the potential of local ecosystems as well as the global and local limits imposed on present and future generations. (Friberg and Hettne, 1982, 22)

The Green approach sees the capitalist societies of the West and the state socialist societies of the East as "two variants of a common corporate industrial culture based on the values of competitive individualism, rationality, growth, efficiency, specialization, centralization and big scale". According to Friberg and Hettne, how these values came about can only be partly explained by economic factors. Rather, "their roots have to be sought, ultimately, in the cultural projects of Western civilization". (Friberg and Hettne, 1982, 36) Thus, for the Greens, the "unbalance between the modern large-scale rationalized sector and the non-modern small-scale personalistic sector" would be an essential element of the predicament of Third World people in all regions of the world.

More generally, their problems would not be simply those arising from capitalism or socialism, but have to do also with "the nation-state, bureaucratic forms of organization, positive science, the patriarchate and the urban way of life". (Friberg and Hettne, 1982, 35) Friberg and Hettne do not wish to eliminate states, only to make them serve the human needs desired by (local) communities better. They see the "Green project" requiring "stronger institutions on the local and regional level", as well as the deemphasis of the state. But they do not present concrete ideas for global institutions which fit the Green approach nor do they indicate whether these institutions should be linked directly to local peoples.

Friberg and Hettne's Green movement transcends single countries and regions. Their "main hypothesis is that the Green movement derives its strength from three rather different sources: *The Traditionalists* who resist modern penetration in the form of commercialization, industrialization, state-building and professionalization. They derive their strength from "non-Western civilizations and religions, old nations and tribes, local communities, kinship groups, peasants and self-employed people, informal economies, women, culture, etc". *Marginalized people* who cannot find a place within the modern sector, "the unemployed, temporary workers, women, youth, the uneducated, workers with soulless jobs, etc". *Post-materialists* who experience some sort of "self-emancipation", often through "opportunities provided by an affluent modern society…They are young, well-educated and committed to non-material values. Their occupations are person-oriented rather than thing-oriented". (Friberg and Hettne, 1982, 42)

Friberg and Hettne perceive these three groups to be at different places in the "center–periphery structure of the world". The traditionalists are to be found primarily in peripheries, the marginalized at the middle level and the post-materialists near the centers. They are now not part of single Green movement. Rather, Friberg and Hettne see all three as potential elements of a worldwide movement.

It is very significant that each of these Indian and Swedish scholars perceive a related set of movements against dominant global and national structures to be a worldwide phenomenon. While focusing on the Indian context, Kothari notes "a more general relevance" and discusses the various dimensions of "new grassroots politics from a global perspective". (Kothari, 1986, 177-183) Sheth perceives a new mode of politics arising across regional, linguistic, cultural and national boundaries. Challenging is the "main hypothesis" of Friberg and Hettne that asserts that the Green movement derives its strength from "traditionalists" in the world periphery, marginalized people in what might be called the "semi-periphery" and "post-materialists" near the world centers.

Another common thesis of these Indian and Swedish scholars is a strong local emphasis. For Friberg and Hettne "the human being or small communities of human beings are the ultimate actors". They emphasize self-reliance and cultural autonomy for local communities. Kothari underlines the importance of a diversity of local peoples movements which are attempting to "open alternative political space". Sheth emphasize local self-determination and the fact that movements are based on a new perspective that "is based, to a large extent, on the day-to-day experience of ordinary people". But both Kothari and Sheth emphasize that "micro-practice" must be guided by "macro thinking" that is significantly shaped by grassroots movements themselves.

4 Three elements of a global visions for peace movements

It is not our intent to imagine a holistic global vision for peace movements. Instead, we are attempting to gain insight on necessary elements of a vision by examination of works on social movements by scholars from a number of countries. Three elements seem to be particularly important. First, the vision must be inclusive of the diversity of themes through which people in various parts of the world are attempting to overcome peacelessness. It is obvious that the list of themes must include those such as nonviolence, economic well-being, social justice, feminism and ecological balance. But there is danger that lists constructed in one part of the world may be inadequate in conveying the perspective of people in other parts of the world.

For example, cultural identity and self-determination may be presumed to be included in a theme such as social justice or human rights, but may receive secondary consideration in the context of these themes. Thus, the list of themes should be open, and inevitably overlapping and messy, in an effort to validly reflect the central concerns of people in all parts of the world.

Second, the vision must expect strong and sustained participation at the grassroots level. It is not difficult to reach the conclusion that most of the peacelessness in the world is associated with lack of grassroots participation. The peacelessness that has been generated by "security states" and their arms races and militarization is strongly associated with lack of participation by people at the grassroots in the attainment of their own security. At the same time, the peacelessness that has been fomented by state "development" plans is rooted in the lack of grassroots participation in formulation of strategies for satisfying basic human needs. But there is still a tendency in much peace research to presume that states must be the prime agents in peace strategies, and to assume that people at the grassroots are incompetent to formulate and implement their own peace strategies. Relevant here is Kothari's call "for a review of ideological positions that continue to locate 'vested interests' in local situations and liberation from them in distant processes – the state, technology, revolutionary vanguards". (Kothari, 1983, 615)

Third, visions are required that specify possibilities for local control over powerful entities, such as states and transnational production, financial, marketing and communications corporations that intrude on local space. Also, what kinds of relationships would there be between local communities in distant parts of the world? New visions of what some would call micro-macro relations are an indispensable part of any useful global vision for peace movements. But at the same time it must be recognized that, for must of us, the possibility of significant impact of local people on macro institutions is "unthinkable". This is because of the way education and socialization have shaped our present perceptions of, and expectations of, micro-macro relations. For this reason this third topic merits somewhat greater attention.

An integral part of disempowerment of the grassroots is the mythology of the state systems that legitimizes activities through which economic-political-military bureaucracies of states dominate the external relations of societies in pursuit of the "national interest". Evidence of the power of the myth is to be found in the fact that virtually all states depend on a small elite to define the "national interest". Products of these "national interest" policies have been arms races, militarized societies, and "development" that does not fulfill human needs but does destroy the environment. How might visions that replace the mythology of the state system provide for local control of the necessary functions of states?

At the same time a significant contributor to peacelessness is the overwhelming presence of transnational production, financial, marketing, communication and service corporations in virtually every city and town in the world – as employer, entertainer, and provider of consumer goods, health care, insurance, news and housing. Literature on world capitalism and dependency has usefully illuminated the multitude of ways in which the lives of local people are dominated by these macro institutions. But these is now increasing concern that the expansion of scholarly attention to the impact of global intrusion on local space has not been accompanied by adequate attentiveness to local response.

Some scholars are now criticizing their colleagues for not contributing knowledge that would be useful in creating political movements for overcoming local dependency. Richard Child Hill, in an interview of the "emergence, consolidation and development" of research on urban political economy, says:

> If, as some scholars imply, the city has become the "weak link" in the world capitalist system, then the most pressing urban research issues today center upon investigation of the conditions under which global-local contradictions...gives rise to political movements and public policies directed toward changing the structure and dynamics of the translocal system. (Hill, 1984, 135)

Craig Murphy makes a similar criticism of world systems research in "a plea for including studies of social mobilization in the world system research program", by asking for "a theory of the role of political consciousness and social mobilization in the dynamic of world capitalism". (Murphy, 1982, 1) Murphy asserts that Stavrianos' popular history of the Third World, *Global Rift* (1981), points the way because he "tells the story of the Third World by constantly focusing om mobilization against capitalism...But the broad strokes of Stavrianos' history need to be filled in by detailed studies of individual political movements, unique and repeated cases of people becoming convinced to act against capitalism...the stuff of actual social mobilization". (Murphy, 1982, 17)

A few scholars are now creating a new literature on local response to macro intrusions. Their research offers insights significant to those who would wish to create useful visions of stronger grassroots peace movements. We will cite only a few examples. (For others, see Alger 1988.)

Sensitive to this issue are two anthropologists working in Central America. Asking that local history in Guatemala be put in global context, Carol A. Smith criticizes anthropologists for recognizing global forces while neglecting "the way in which local systems affect the regional structures, economic and political, on which global forces play". At the same time, she observes that scholars in other social sciences "are even more likely to view local systems as the passive recipients of global processes". (Smith, 1985, 109-110) Based on his work in Nicaragua, Richard Adams acknowledges the impacts of global capitalist expansion. Yet he observes that it is necessary to recognize that local "life and culture continue to yield new emergent social entities, new adaptive forms brought into being in order to pursue survival and reproduction both through and in spite of the specific work of capitalism". (Adams, 1981, 7) Yet another anthropologists, John W. Bennett, writing in the context of "microcosm-macrocosm relationships" in North American agrarian society, has warned against unfounded assumptions about the domination of the local community by external influences and directs attention to the ways "the local spatial system retain many if its 'traditional' institutions and utilizes these to manipulate and control the external forces". (Bennett, 1967, 442)

Wallerstein notes that "the household as an income-pooling unit can be seen as a fortress both of accommodation to and resistance to the patterns of labor-force allocation favored by accumulators". (Wallerstein, 1984, 21) His conclusion is supported by illuminating studies of household in Oaxaca, Mexico and Davao City, Philippines, that offers insight on the capacity of households to resist efforts by the state to "help" marginal and poor workers to cope with the intrusion of world wide economic processes into their daily lives.

In this study, Hackenberg, Murphy and Selby criticize dependency theorists, and implicitly most world systems theorists, by noting that their kind of theory is "less interested in the reactions and strivings of the exploited than it is in delineating the historical, sociological, cultural and economic forces that coadjust to exploit them". Because dependency theory portrays the urban household as "fairly helpless", the authors "take leave of dependency theory" and depict the household as a vital institution that endeavors to protect its interests by doing battle with state programs that would undermine the integrity of the household by "opportunities generated by development" that would exploit "the desires of some household members to better themselves economically at the expense of other members". (Hackenberg, Murphy and Selby, 1984, 189-190)

Insights on visions that explicate local control over intrusive macro processes can also be gained by closer observation of increasingly creative efforts of local people to "Think globally and Act locally". Relevant here are local campaigns too numerous to mention. (For more detailed treatment see Alger and Mendlovitz, 1987; Alger, 1988.) They include local government actions to establish nuclear-free zones, to disinvest in corporations doing business in South Africa, and to offer sanctuary to immigrants who the national immigration service wishes to deport. This new paradigm is also reflected in the European centered "Towns and Development" programs in which European towns and cities have established programs for offering development assistance to Third World towns and cities. (Kussendrayer, 1988) In some cases, as in Bruges, Belgium, this involves the appointment of an Alderman for Development. Evidence of the growth in these kinds of activities can be found in the new *Bulletin of Municipal Foreign Policies*. Still missing is a more holistic vision of the implications of fragmentary efforts to identify and act on the local policy implications of growing world wide involvements manifest in the daily lives of people in local settlements.

5 Implications for peace research

Finally, what are the implications of these conclusions for peace research? This is another way of saying: Where do peace researchers fit in out global visions for peace movements? This is a fourth necessary element in global visions for peace movements. Sheth, in an already quoted passage, aptly describes the challenge that confronts peace researchers:

> It is the dialectic between micro-practice and macro-thinking that will actualize a new politics of the future...In brief a macro-vision is the prime need of these groups and movements, and this can be satisfied only by a growing partnership between activists and intellectuals in the process of social transformation. (Sheth 1983, 386)

Other researchers too are saying that we must employ new methodologies in the creation of knowledge of value to the grassroots. Catalin Mamali has succinctly described the connection between research and participation by observing that "the conscious participation of the members of a social community in its evolution process, *also depends upon the level and quality of participation of its members (specialists and laymen) in knowing the reality they live in"*. Pointing out that each member of a community has a double cognitive status, that of observed and that of observer, he notes that prevalent research practice inhibits "'the subjects' natural observer status". Thus he concludes that a "just distribution of social knowledge cannot be reached unless its process of production is democratized". (Mamali, 1979, 13-14)

Grassroots peace movements are a serious challenge to present research agendas throughout the world. While necessary evidence is not available for making an authoritative worldwide assessment, it appears that grassroots movements in all continents have grown more rapidly than the capacity of researchers to observe and interpret their activities. Kinhide Mushakoji has observed that "peace research at the grassroots level should make special efforts to create new paradigms because if has been one of the weakest points of conventional peace research". Mushakoji advocates research based on the center–periphery paradigm, criticizing traditional peace researchers for having a "tendency to focus on the danger of potential war between the superpowers". (Mushakoji, 1978, 186) In other words Mushakoji is asking that grassroots peace movements be put in the paradigm so that the impact of centers on the grassroots be made transparent, enabling individuals and groups at the grassroots to perceive the concrete activities through which this influence is transmitted. At the same time the efforts of grassroots movements to overcome peacelessness must be a part of the paradigm so that grassroots movements can use this knowledge for enhancing their potential.

Mushakoji also stresses the importance of basing grassroots peace research on the values of people living in grassroots communities, overcoming the tendency to import values in research paradigms developed in the centers. He further advocates that peace researchers should seek out the problems of local peace activists and address these problems in their research, feeding back the results to local activists, receiving feedback again and advancing with another round of research.

Mushakoji pushes even further in urging departure from the traditional research methodologies of academic centers, advocating that peace research at the grassroots level should approach local values through an organized effort of endogenous peace-learning. This conscientization process, he says, "must be developed in such a way that it deepens the awareness of 'peacelessness' ". In envisaging peace researchers as working with activists in the building of a peaceful grassroots community, he joins Paolo Freire in advocating that researchers and the people become co-investigators. (Paolo Freire, 1971, 97) Mushakoji cites as an example of the kind of feedback process he is advocating research in India on the practice of nonviolent resistance. (For fuller treatment see Alger, 1987.)

References

Adams, Richard N.: "The Dynamics of Societal Diversity: Notes from Nicaragua for a Sociology of Survival", *American Enthnologist* 8, (1), 1981, 1-20.

Alger, Chadwick F.: "A Grassroots Approach to Life in Peace: Self-Determination in Overcoming Peacelessness", *Bulletin of Peace Proposals,* Vol. 18, No. 3, 375-392.

Alger, Chadwick F.: "Perceiving, Analyzing and Coping with the Local-Global Nexus", *International Social Science Journal,* 1988 (in press).

Alger, Chadwick F. and Mendlovitz, Saul H.: "Grassroots Initiatives: The challenge of Linkages" in Mendlovitz and Walker, eds.: *Towards a Just World Peace: Perspectives from Social Movements,* Butterworths, London, 1987, 333-362.

Bennett, John W.: "Microcosm-Macrocosm Relationships in North American Agrarian Society", *American Anthropologist,* Vol. 69 (1), 1967, 441-454.

Brand, Karo Werner; Busser D., and Rucht, D.: *Aubruch Eine Andere Gessellschaft, Neue Soziale Bewegungen in der Bundesrepublik,* Campus, Frankfurt, 1983.

De Deken, Johan J.: "A Socio-Political Profile of the current Peace Movement in Flanders", *Vredesonderzoek,* Interfacultari Overlegorggan Voor Vredesonderzoek van de Vrije Universiteit, Brussels, No. 1, 1988.

Freire, Paolo: *Pedagogy for the Oppressed,* Herder and Herder, New York, 1971.

Friberg, Mats and Hettne, Björn: "The Greening of the World: Towards a Non-Deterministic Model of Global Processes", University if Gothenburg, Sweden (xerox), 1982.

Hackenberg, Robert; Murphy, Arthur D. and Selby, Henry A.: "The Urban Household in Dependent Development" in Nettin, Robert McC; Welk, Richard R. and Arnould, Eric J. eds: *Households: Comparative and Historical Studies of the domestic Group*, University of California Press, Berkeley, 1984.

Hill, Richard Child: "Urban Political Economy: Emergency, Consolidation and Development", in Smith, Peter ed.: *Cities in Transformation: Class, Capital, State,* Sage, Beverly Hills, 1984.

Kothari, Rajni: "Party and State in our Times: The Rise if Non-Party Political Formations", *Alternatives,* IX, 1983, 595-618.

Kothari, Rajni: "Masses, Classes and the State", in Mendlovitz and Walker, eds.: *Toward a Just World Peace: Perspectives for Social Movements,* Butterworths, London, 1987, 387-403.

Kussendrayer, Nico: "Towns and Development: NGO and Local Authority Joint Action for North-South Cooperation.Casestudies from Belgium, Germany, the Netherlands and the United Kingdom", second edition, The Hague: Towns and Development Campaign Secretariat, 1988.

Mamali, Catalin: "Societal Learning and Democratization of the Social Research Process", Bucharest:,Research Center for Youth Problems, 1979.

Mendlovitz, Saul H. and Walker, R.B.J. eds.: *Toward a Just World Peace: Perspectives for Social Movements,* Butterworths, London, 1987.

Milbrath, Lester: "Making Connections: The Common Roots Giving Rise the the Environmental, Feminist and Peace Movements", Annual Meeting of the International Society for Political Psychology, July, 1988.

Murphy, Craig: "Understanding the World Economy in Order to Change It: A Plea for Including Studies of Social Mobilization in the World System Research Program", International Studies Association convention, 1982.

Mushakoji, Kinhide; "Peace Research as an International Learning Process", *International Studies Quarterly,* 22, No. 2, June, 1978, 173-194.

Offe, Claus: "New Social Movements: Challenging the Boundaries of Institutional Politics", *Social Research,* Vol. 52, No. 4, Winter, 1985.

Sheth, D.L.: "Grass-Roots Stirrings and the Future of Politics", *Alternatives*, IX, 1983, 1-24.

Sheth, D.L.: "Alternative Development as Political Practice", in Mendlovitz and Walker, eds.: *Toward a Just World Peace: Perspectives for Social Movements,* Butterworths, London, 1987, 235-251.

Smith, Joan; Wallerstein, Immanuel and Evers, Hans-Dieter eds.: *Households and the World Economy,* Sage, Beverly Hills, 1984.

Smith, Carol A.: "Local History in Global Context: Social and Economic Transitions in Western Guatemala", in DeWalt and Pelto eds., 1985, 83-120.

United Nation University, Memo for Panel of UN Experts, 'Life in Peace-3', January 1986.

Wallerstein, Immanuel: "Household Structures and Labor-Force Formation in the Capitalist World-Economy", in Smith, Wallerstein, Evers eds.: *Households and the World Economy,* Sage, Beverly Hills, 1984, 17-22.

Peace Movements

in Eastern Europe

Radmila Nakarada
Institute of International Labour Movements, Belgrade

There are some concepts in human life that seem non-problematic and self-evident in their desirability, in their positive connotation. However, life furnishes us with a series of paradoxes even when concepts such as freedom, human rights and peace are concerned. In a particular historical moment in the evolution of a society, in a particular set of social circumstances, life demonstrates the relativity of even undeniable values. For instance, in a situation of grave economic crisis, the unquestionable desirability, self-evident positive connotation of human rights, democratization is tarnished, at least in the eyes of the victims of the crisis. Or, individuals may gain more rights, but society may not survive in a rational manner, the processes of democratization. It may open up for a series of retrograde tendencies, e.g. for nationalistic "wars" and religious fundamentalism, that threaten the very existence of society. That is, enlarging the scope of rights, one is not activating only the constructive, enriching social energies, but also disintegrative ones. An overload may be created, due to the nature of the society, its previous erosion, insufficient organic links, turning democratization into a self-defeating tendency.

Eastern European societies, particularly those undergoing reforms, are an arena of such paradoxes. In the Soviet Union for instance, the economic crisis has turned dramatically worse since the process of perestroika was initiated, albeit not due to perestroika itself. Citizens stand in endless queues for almost all essential consumer goods. This has created the feeling that the past was better, including the Stalin era, for there was more existential stability. Life itself, and not a repressive leadership, may reduce democratic aspirations to a demand for a non-humiliating standards of existence. This may result, on the level of social organization, in the combination of a liberal economy and an authoritarian political order.

In multinational countries, like the Soviet Union and Yugoslavia, democratization means furthering the principle of national autonomy and sovereignty. However, in reality this has unleashed a series of separatistic movements that threaten not only the stability of these individual countries, but global and European security. Also, a phenomenon of national democracy is appearing, where a democratic framework is sought only for one's own people and human rights are defined primarily within the interests of one's own nation. In several cases, for instance, in the Soviet Union (in the Baltic Republics, Ukraine, Moldavia) the equal status for one's own language was sought at the level of the whole country, while the same principles was not respected in one's own republic.

Furthermore, life demonstrates that democracy is not only an ethical question, but a matter of knowledge and wisdom. An overriding majority would agree today that democracy is a political and developmental necessity for Eastern Europe. However, problems appear when the general, undeniable value of democracy to be translated into concrete political steps and solutions and answers to the following questions must be found: how to change existing institutions in a non-violent manner, transcend the apathy and mistrust of citizens, neutralize the repressive apparatus, gain the support of the nomenclature, pacify the extremists in the opposition and dogmatics in the party, attain viable social compromises, transcend the existing order without ending up in "totalitarian anti-communism", or in the explosions of ethnical conflicts.[1] These are not only problems of intentions, power and will but also of (insufficient) knowledge, of missing links between general civilizational formulas and their concrete implementation.

Peace is another concept which against the background of Eastern European reality is subjected to a series of unexpected relativizations. If any concept seems unquestionable and crucial it is peace, the first and foremost precondition of life itself. However, the question of peace has recently become the object of paradigmatic and political controversies, as well as bitter misunderstandings between the independent Western and the Eastern social movements. The Western movements considered the struggle for peace an unquestionable priority, an overdetermining precondition of all social processes, while the Eastern Europeans, attributed such a significance to the struggle for freedom and human rights. It took many years to come to a mutual recognition that these two values, crucial for the modern age, are interdependent, indivisible, and that the agenda of both movements can be broadened to incorporate simultaneously issues of democracy and peace. It took many years for the evolution of independent peace movements in Eastern Europe which articulate this interconnection in a dedicated manner, for example in Poland: "Freedom and Peace"; in Czechoslovakia: "Independent Peace Association"; in Yugoslavia: "The People for Peace Culture".[2] Previously, the issue of peace, if taken up, was discussed under the auspice of other social movements.

1 Reticence about peace

The evolution in the relationship of East European movements toward peace can be divided into three phases. The first phase (late seventies, early eighties) was characterized by a reticence about peace. The explanation for the reticence about peace as an issue, the stress on human rights as the precondition for dignified peace, is given by one of the most famous Czech activists and playwriters, Vaclav Havel. According to him, peace has been devoid of meaning in Eastern Europe because it is prey to ideological manipulation, because it presupposes an anti-Western stand (i.e. antidemocratic stand), because the individual risk is great when touching the realm of state security, because it may be a new utopian promise or a new version of legitimating violence to life, and because peace is a poetic means of colonizing human consciousness.[3]

It remains unclear why freedom and human rights are not as much the prey to ideological manipulation as peace is, why the risk of fighting for freedom is smaller than fighting for peace, when Havel himself has been in and out of jail because of his human rights activities. It is unclear why one should forget the immense violence practiced in the name of freedom, or utilization of the poetry of freedom as means of colonizing human consciousness. According to my opinion, the source of previous reticence about peace is not to be sought only in the indicated realms, but also in the fact that the drama of socialist societies (in terms of betrayal of ideals and repression of individuals) as well as the drama of the banished democracy, has transformed peace into a relative abstract, unconvincing problem. Caught in their own reality, their own fate, discouraged by the indifference of Western peace movements to the internal repression in the socialist societies, the East European activists did not become a member in the movement for peace with a universal, trans-ideological meaning.

It is interesting to note that a similar kind of reticence to peace was present (and still is), among the leftist movements in Latin America. They considered détente, disarmament, and unimpressive achievement by the privileged regions of the world – since their own impoverishment and hunger was an ongoing but unrecognized genocide – a never-ending state of war, that merits little attention from the self-centered over-developed world.

The period of reticence, lacked the recognition that among the Western social movements elements of a new consciousness was appearing, beyond divisions, beyond the two dominant and hostile ideologies. It was a reflection of a broader shift in human thinking. This shift was the result of a combination of new problems, new awareness, new possibilities. The disappointing achievements of liberalism and socialism, the danger of exterminism, as well as the possibility of solidarity and dialogue and cooperation towards a viable and desirable, more just and ecologically sane future, gave new social movements – peace movements included – a trans-ideological and trans-class aura. The failure to realize this is illustrated among else in an unusually bitter reaction to the slogan that appeared among the Western peace movement: "Better red than dead". It was interpreted by Vaclav Havel and F. Feher, for instance, as a total defeat, as a testimony of how freedom has become so irrelevant that no one is willing to die for it.[4] Life has been reduced to mere biological survival, and in the shadow of doomsday (a fear nurtured intentionally in order to minimize the importance of freedom) dignified human existence has become of secondary importance. However, the slogan does not necessarily symbolize the total defeat of freedom, but the idea that no ideology is worth dying for. The growing realization that both grand projects of social development have been disappointing resulted in the view that citizens should seed a trans-ideological option, not renouncing the values of meaningful human life, but asserting it beyond the two hostile and unfulfilling ideologies.

2 Democratic peace

A second phase covers the period when peace and human rights became explicitly linked, mutually determining issues. The Czechoslovak independent movement Charter 77 began stressing, since the early eighties, the indivisibility of peace and freedom, the inextricably intertwining of peace and human rights. For instance, Jaroslav Sabata, in a dialogue with E.P. Thompson, launched the concept of *democratic peace,* underlining that peace is not only the absence of war, of weapons, but also of political repression, social tension.[5]

In 1985, Charter 77 in the "Prague Appeal" linked peace issue with the Helsinki process, and influenced the Western peace movements to consider the Helsinki accords as a framework for promoting peace issues. This resulted in a genuine East-West dialogue, the outcome of which was, among else the memorandum "Giving Real Life to the Helsinki Accords". A number of Easter and Western activist agreed: "A lasting peace can only be obtained by overcoming the various political, economic and social causes of aggression and violence in international relations as well as in the internal affairs of states. A comprehensive democratization of states and societies would create conditions favorable to this aim."[6]

This was a moment of fruitful East–West dialogue, a moment of mutual solidarity and trust. Besides the dialogue between the Eastern and Western movements the issue of democratic peace has initiated a series of joint actions, primarily in the form of statements, and appeals, between East European countries. There have been protests against the invasion of Czechoslovakia, repeated on the occasion of its 10th and 20th anniversary,[7] against the stationing of Soviets missiles on the Czech and East German territory, and against the imprisonment of conscientious objectors.

However, the more elaborate articulation of the idea of democratic peace demonstrates two features. First, while the linkage of peace and freedom is prevailing, it is not a homogeneous or a consistent stand. There are those in East Europe who continues to uphold the idea that human rights have priority in "solving a number of world problems, including war and peace"[8]. Similarly, the Charter 77 letter to the Moscow seminar on human rights, expresses the authors conviction that the "respect for human rights and freedom is one of the basic preconditions of the policy of peace and cooperation between nations and states"[9]. They protest against all military interventions, military measures (in Poland) and demand the withdrawal of Soviet troops from Czechoslovakia, but the thrust of the argument remains that the single most important criteria of trustworthiness of states involved in the process of disarmament is their recognition of civic and human rights. Secondly, even though democratic peace became a shared concern of the Eastern and Western movements, and even though the removal of the Yalta division, the dismantling of the military blocs and the creation of a united, nuclear-free, democratic Europe became a common goal, the concrete elaborations are not identical. They again reflect the different *realities,* different deprivations of those concerned with democracy and peace. In Eastern Europe, peace is primarily understood as *internal* peace, peace between the state, society and citizens, as a universal right, "the right to pacifism", the right to conscientious objection, as a problem of withdrawal of foreign (Soviet) troops, and *finally* as conventional and nuclear disarmament.

The desire and the demand for internal peace is articulated in many different ways. Vaclav Havel has probably voiced this concern in the most convincing manner: "Without free, self-respecting and autonomous citizens, there can be no free and independent nations. Without internal peace, that is, peace among citizens and between citizens and the state, there can be no guarantee of external peace: a state that ignores the will and the rights of its citizens can offer no guarantee that it will respect the will and the rights of other peoples, nations and states...Suppressing the natural rights of citizens and peoples does not secure peace – quite the contrary, it endangers it. A lasting peace and disarmament can only be the work of free people."[10] Similarly, the East German "Peace and Human Rights" initiative explains that peace is always a process of internal *socio-political transformation.* In order to secure the internal presuppositions for peace in their own society they consider the establishment of constitutionalism and democratization two major tasks.[11] Others have expressed the demand for internal peace in the form of globally oriented slogan, concrete critical political references, visions of democratic Europe, presuppositions in international trust. Thus, the slogan of Jan Urban of Charter 77, "A world without tanks", was promoted by other peace movements in Easter Europe, among else the Moscow trust group, as an expression of, as L. Bogoraz explains, "our relationship to both the armed interference in other countries and to the repressive methods in internal politics"[12]. And, Lennon's song "Give peace a chance", is translated by the Czech Lennonists into a condemnation of injustice and violence not only from outside the state but also from *within*.[13]

Criticizing the insincerity of Jaruzelski's peace initiatives, Adam Michnik forcefully suggest that the general could "make a genuine peace initiative by seeking a peaceful rapprochement *with his own nation*".[14] (Emphasizes by R.N.)

In depicting the conditions for creating a democratic Europe, Jaroslav Sabata emphasizes the crucial importance of attaining internal peace in East Europe. According to him, genuine anti-militaristic democracy (i.e. democratic peace), can not prevail in the whole of Europe if a radical anti-bureaucratic change does not take place in the *Eastern bloc*. "This is the only way the concept of anti-militaristic democracy could become a legitimate part of European democracy."[15] Finally, discussing the conditions of establishing *international trust,* global peace, the members of the Moscow Trust group have emphasized the necessity of respecting human rights *at home*.[16]

All of these elaborations of *internal peace,* contain a profound drama, painful limitations, unjust deprivations of socialist societies. They are echoes of many tragic individual fates. They represent a protest against repression, the rule of the party that replaced the rule of law, the domination of lies and humiliation of individuality. Equally, they are an articulation of accumulated civilizational aspirations, an outcry for a more desirable future.

Beside the general issue of internal peace the Eastern European peace movements, as well as other independent social movements, have intensively focused on a particular question – the right to conscientious objection, the right to pacifism. Conscientious objection is promoted as a universal right, embodying simultaneously the freedom of conviction and expression. The promotion of the right to conscientious objection has two particularly important aspects. First, amidst the torment of arms race and militarization it is a means of preserving the seeds of peace in the soul of each human being, an essential "ingredient" of the humanization and demilitarization of societies. Second, promoting the right to conscientious objection implies the limitation of the state's sovereignty over the individual. As Miklos Haraszti, points out, obtaining this right is the acknowledgement that state's sovereignty over the individual can not be absolute.[17]

The issue of conscientious objection has been proclaimed as the embodiment of the Helsinki spirit. At several occasions this has served as the basis for joint Eastern European protests and appeals of activists. Thus a joint appeal was addressed to the CSCE Conference i Vienna, protesting against governments that do not respect the individuals right's right to follow the dictates of their own conscience. "War and the suppression of the rights of individuals go hand in hand... As long as people who refuse to consider other nations as enemies are prosecuted, détente cannot be firmly established in a divided Europe. Governments that demand that other governments renounce violence publicly, while they themselves imprison those who reject it, cannot be trusted."[18]

The peace movements in Hungary, Yugoslavia, as well as the Polish "Freedom and Peace" movement, have recently succeeded in legiting conscientious objection. The laws have been changed, allowing alternative military service for all those who, on the base of their (primarily religious) convictions, refuse to serve the army.

Concerning disarmament, the East European peace movements are naturally supportive of all initiatives in this direction. Without exception they considered the INF treaty a positive international achievement.[19] In general, the concern for global militarization, the support for disarmament and the dismantling of military blocs are immersed in the concrete reality of these societies, in the relations with and within the Warsaw Pact, as well as toward internal military structures.

Thus, the general concerns are translated into specific demands for democratization, in the initial phase, and then for abolition if the Warsaw Pact, the reduction of conventional arms, and the withdrawal of all Soviet troops from the Warsaw Pact countries, beginning with Czechoslovakia and Hungary where military interventions took place in 1968 and 1956. Internally, articulated demands for public disclosure of military budgets, for cuts in military expenditure, public control of the army apparatus and its decision-making processes, are becoming a major aspect of the democratization of these societies.

3 Reforms in East Europe and peace

The unprecedented reforms initiated in the Soviet Union, the restructuring; perestroika, that has brought change in the internal and international framework, has encouraged the reform movements in other East European countries, primarily in Poland and Hungary. The suspension of the Brezhnev doctrine, the recognition of national sovereignty and the right to ones own road to socialism has been particularly encouraging. The shadow of external intervention has, if not totally disappeared, diminished sufficiently to create the social space for the revitalization of the civil societies.

Thus, the peace initiatives of the states (the détente from above), as well as the internal peace initiatives from below such as changing laws to allow alternative military service, promoting human rights, legitimating pluralism as a political and economic principle, have resulted in the partial fulfillment of some of the aims of peace movements. Thus, the new phase entails the widening of the agenda of peace movements, both as a response to new problems and as a means of revitalizing the movements themselves.

In the newly created social space, demands of peace movements are reaching the deeper foundations of peace as an irreversible process. They are spontaneously problematizing the demonstrated links between social reforms, economic relations, ecological problems and peace. From military and political demands the movements are moving in the direction of social, economic and ecological ones. New economic relations between the East and West, including the necessity of a new Marshall plan and of transforming the world economic order, are rapidly becoming central concerns of peace movements. Linking peace, freedom and bread, is not a sign of loosing identity, but of a more profound understanding of the preconditions of irreversible peace.

The new phase breeds new coalitions and alliances between movements and unions and between movements and reformists within the Party. This is the natural outcome of new demands, that lead to new coalitions, resulting in new energies of the movements themselves.

Furthermore, initiatives for creating new transnational institutions are launched. One of the most important is the proposal for a Peace Parliament in Prague, a forum for NGOs, later renamed as the European Citizen's Assembly. It was proposed by Charter 77 and supported by the European Nuclear Disarmament, END. The spirit of the movement is expressed in its proposal: "We do not wish to destroy the existing political and economic structures in Europe but to further develop them. We wish to work for mutual convergence of all European countries. To achieve this we need to create new structures – institutional ties in all spheres of social life – to bring about an integral process of democratic changes in Europe. And independent peace institutions is an important element of this process." This initiative is part of building a transnational civil society, legitimizing the citizens as a transnational category, institutionally overcoming the consequences of the Cold war and creating a forum for the resolution of common problems, "where the right to self-organization can be asserted and protected throughout Europe". It is a means of realizing and advancing the democratic potential of détente.[20]

4 Problems and limitations

Some of the problems facing peace movements stem from their spontaneous evolution. As the representative of Polish "Freedom and Peace" movement, Jacek Czaputowics indicates, the fact that the movement has no structure, makes its representation and formulation of goals difficult.[21] Second, new requirements have emerged, both in terms of issues and modes of action, and the framework of a movement like "Freedom and Peace" is too restricted. Third, a problem shared by almost all social movements in Eastern Europe, with the exception of "Solidarity" is their narrow social base and low following. In spite of the fact that their social importance by far exceeds the numbers of followers, the factor cannot be ignored as a limitation.[22]

Other problems stem from the repressive character of socialist societies, that force peace movements into inhibiting alliances, for instance with the Church. This problem has been described by the members of the East German "Peace and Human Rights Initiative". They have remained independent from both the State and Church, being critical of the compromising stand the Church had on some of the most fundamental issues. They have refused to accept the Church as the substitute for the public realm, seeking true public space for self-organization and individual initiative. Renouncing the protection of the Church and engaging in independent activities has resulted in severe state repression towards its members.[23]

A series of limitations of the peace movements evolve from the paradigms they adhere to. Eastern European peace movements are not sufficiently critical of the Western establishment and are upset with the criticism the movements in the West make of their own society. They consider this a luxury when compared with the reality within which they are struggling. They do not realize that an anti-bureaucratic reform in the East is not sufficient for the democratization of Europe. Broadening and deepening democracy in the West is also necessary.

Peace movements adhere to various ahistorical evaluations. The concept of Central Europe for instance, is usually taken only in its positive aspect, while its authoritarian heritage is conveniently forgotten. The present is perceived as a total historical discontinuity due to the Soviet occupation and not as something that has to do with one's own past as well. Sobering is M. Simecka's warning: "It's far pleasanter to pass oneself off as a guiltless nation which would show the world if it only got the chance. I just think that it serves a purpose – of only a therapeutic one – to be reminded that a lot of the evil was our own creation, and one of the reasons why the influence of the 'other civilization' was so effective was because, to a certain extent, we provided it with fertile soil." Equally sobering is Jaroslav Sabata's analyses of the role reformist Czech communists played in the breakdown of the Prague Spring.

Caught by the drama of their own reality, the peace movements share also a specific Eurocentrism. Their own drama overshadows the drama of the Third World, the tragedy of repression and poverty in e.g. Latin American countries.

Finally, the economy and its relation to freedom and peace is not fully comprehended. This is expressed either in the form of overemphasing political problems, unrealistic expectations that political reforms will automatically result in economic changes and betterment. Or, it is taken for granted that the free market represents a solution to all problems. In other words, in terms of envisioning economic reforms there are no other problems to be considered, other than the implementation of market mechanisms.

5 Conclusions

Peace movements are manyfold things, between the East and West, between the reality and potentiality of individual societies, between memory and modernity, pain and hope, the old and new paradigms. At the same time, movements will share the predicaments of their own societies.

The current ferment is demanding unambiguous acknowledgement that socialist countries are not monolithic as individual societies, nor as as bloc. Furthermore, their transformation potential differs. One can distinguish countries that are struggling hard to remain unchanged, those that are interested in very limited changes, primarily economic ones, those that are undergoing changes in a retrograde direction, and those that are attempting radical political and economic changes. How movements will survive in the reformist countries, amidst the newly created social space and new hostilities within the civil society, depends on their wisdom, creativity and responsibility. For they are now active participants in the creation of the tomorrow of their society. How movements will survive in the non-reforming countries depends on the mystery of human courage and transnational solidarity. Repression will color the loves of still many who continue to be actively concerned with democratic peace. Both will share the uncertainty of reforms, and as unconvincing as it seems, and of repression.

Notes and references

1) Some experts believe the Soviet Union could be the first victim of ethnic nationalism (Malcolm Oross).

2) Freedom and Peace (WIP) focuses om the militarization of the Polish society and the right to alternative military service. It has committed itself to seeking nonviolent solutions to social problems. It is the only Polish opposition group that has included a struggle against the nuclear threats among its goals. The Independent Peace Association defines its aims as overcoming distrust by openness, transcending the ideology of the "Other" as enemy, promoting education based on the respect of human life, acknowledging the right to conscientious objection and supporting all step leading ti disarmament. In Yugoslavia, the People for Peace Culture takes up issues of militarism and advocates the right to conscientious objection.

3) Vaclav Havel, *The Anatomy of a Reticence,* The Charter 77 foundation, Stockholm, 1986.

4) Ibid.

5) See *From Below,* A Helsinki Watch Report, Oct. 1987, pp. 8. It is interesting to note, that while independent peace movements did not exist, the Charter 77 articulated the most persuasive ideas concerning peace and freedom and had a profound impact on the dialogue with the Western peace movements.

6) Quoted according to *From Below,* op. cit. pp. 239–258. The Moscow trust group states: "It is impossible to speak about peace without also discussing human rights issues. In the same way, it is unacceptable to be involved with the struggle for human rights while relegating to second place the problem of preserving peace, and ultimately, the survival of humankind." *Ukrainian Peace News,* Vol. 1, No. 3/4, 1987, pp. 8.

7) A joint Eastern European statement to commemorate the 20th anniversary of the Warsaw Pact invasion of Czechoslovakia was signed by 120 leading activist from almost 25 different group, coming from five countries, including the Soviet Union. *East European Reporter,* (EER), Vol. 3, No. 3, 1988, pp. 59.

8) Lariss Bogoraz, in Historic International Human Rights Conference in Moscow, *Across Frontiers,* Vol. 4, No. 2/3, 1988, pp. 13.

9) Ibid. pp 14.

10) Vaclav Havel, op. cit. pp. 23.

11) See Self-Portrayal of the "Initiative Peace and Human Rights", in *Bulletin of the European Network for East-West Dialogue,* No. 1-2, 1988, pp. 32.

12) Quoted according to the Historic International Human Rights Conference in Moscow, *Across Frontiers,* Vol. 4, No. 2/3, 1988.

13) The Lennonists have demanded the removal of nuclear arms and the Soviet troops from Czechoslovakia, the right to alternative military service and the release of all political prisoners.

14) An interview with Adam Michnik, *East European Reporter*, Vol.3, No.2, pp 25.

15) Jaroslav Sabata: "Gorbachev's Reforms and the Future of Europe, *East European Reporter,* op. cit. pp. 8.

16) See Resolutions and other documents of the Moscow Independent Seminar on Humanitarian Problems, A Helsinki Watch Report, Aug. 1988, pp. 9-13.

17) Miklos Hereszti: "If Eastern Europeans Object to Military Service", *New York Times*, Aug. 15, 1987.

18) Joint Appeal of Eastern Europeans to the CSCE Conference in Vienna On Conscientious Objection, in *Bulletin Of the European Network for East-West Dialogue*, No. 1/2, 1988, pp.58.

19) See Resolution and other documents of the Moscow Independent Seminar on Humanitarian Problems, A Helsinki Watch Report, Aug. 1988, pp. 9 and the Declaration of Independent Peace Association issued in May 1988.

20) Proposal for a Peace Parliament in Prague, *East European Reporter,* op. cit. pp 20. See also the END editorial of Mary Kaldor, *END*, Issue 37, 1989.

21) The Polish Movement, "Freedom and Peace" in a New Phase of its Development, An Interview with Jacek Czeputowicz, in *Bulletin of the European Network for East-West Dialogue,* No. 1-2/88, pp. 62-64.

22) Vaclav Havel explains that Charter 77 draws its strength "from the truth it articulate – the truth which is on the whole shared by society". Interview with Havel, *East European Reporter,* No.2, op. cit. pp. 3.

23) Reinhard Weishuhn, A New Quality of Independent Activities, in *Bulletin of the European Network for East-West Dialogue,* No. 1-2/88, pp. 28, sheds light on the problems the East German movement had with Church.

24) M. Simicka, Interview, Obsah, Prague, 1986. Jaroslav Sabata: "Invasion of own goal?", *East European Reporter,* No. 3. op. cit. pp. 3-6.

Sociological Implications of Hiroshima and the Anti-Nuclear Weapons Movement

Shingo Shibata
Faculty of Integrated Arts and Sciences,
Hiroshima University

1 Sociological implications of Hiroshima and Nagasaki

Most people know what happened in Hiroshima and Nagasaki in 1945, but not many have considered its implications for sociology and sociologists. In my opinion, the sociological implications of the nuclear destructions of the two cities can be summarized as follows:

1 Complete destruction of a society

I will not set out in detail the number of people massacred by those two atomic bombs, but more than 200,000 had died by the end of that year, 1945, and the greater part of the total society of both cities was completely destroyed; homes, workplaces, markets hospitals, schools, kindergartens, temples, churches, the very community itself. The entire milieu for sustaining human life, including the regional community and support systems, was totally demolished.[1] It was a crime not only of massive genocide but also sociocide and vandalism. The society itself, as an object of sociological research was destroyed, and sociologists, themselves actors in sociological study, were wiped out. As one of the important concepts of sociology, we think of "social disorganization" or "social disintegration". Both these terms designate the general conception of socio-pathological phenomena. About twenty years ago I had an opportunity to do some sociological research about how U.S. military forces deliberately forced "social disorganization" on Vietnamese society.[2] It was one of the most brutal forms of "social disorganization" in history. The nuclear destruction of Hiroshima and Nagasaki, as another form of this, should still be carefully studied today, because it is not merely an event of the past but a present potentiality. One of the most urgent tasks of sociologists in this nuclear age is to study the sociological aspects of nuclear disorganization, viz., sociocide.

In connection with this thesis, I think all will agree that the study of crime has played an important role in the development of sociology. The following sociologists are found among well-known scholars who engaged in criminal studies: J. G. Tarde, E. Durkheim, W. I. Thomas, F. T. Tönnies, A. H. Cantril, F. H. Sutherland and others. If a small crime or small criminal group is a subject of such important studies for sociology, how could it be that the more, nay, the *most* evil war and genocidal crimes and the greatest violence of groups such as nuclear-armed forces are not a subject for sociology? Already we can cite E. A. Cohen's *Human Behaviour in the Concentration Camp* (1953) as a study of Nazi crimes of genocide, and C. W. Mills' *Power Elite* (1956) and *Listen, Yankee* (1960) as sociological analyses of U.S. crimes of aggression.

Two decades ago I also proposed a sociology of war crimes, applying it to the U.S. war crimes in Vietnam.[3] As already suggested, the war crimes of Hiroshima and Nagasaki included all kind of killing: homicide, infanticide, matricide, patricide, genocide, biocide, ecocide and so on. With a deep understanding of such a completely new aspect of the nuclear age, Prof. John Somerville, one of the really pioneering anti-nuclear sociologists and philosophers, proposed the new word, "omnicide".[4] I agree fully with him and would like to propose a new genre of sociology, that is, a sociology of omnicide, which could be the most appropriate sociological expression of nuclear destruction.

2 Sociological implications and studies of hibakusha

The atomic bomb exterminated not only several "societies" and "communities", but was an instrument of the "delayed genocide" of the atomic bombed, as well as "futurocide", if I may coin a word for it, inflicting suffering upon generations to follow. By the end of 1984, i.e. 39 years after the first nuclear omnicide, a total of 367,344 persons had been granted hibakusha (atomic survivors) certificates. Since some have not received certificates because of possible discrimination in marriage and employment, the actual number of hibakusha should be considered higher than that. It should also be noted that the concept, "hibakusha" consists of three genres as follows: a) the directly atomic bombed, b) the indirectly atomic bombed who suffered radiation from the radioactive black rain, entering both cities within a short time after the bombing, helping the directly atomic bombed and cremating the dead, and c) those who were children in the wombs at atomic bomb victim mothers.

Many of the hibakusha have lost members of their families through injuries or sickness caused directly or indirectly by the bombing, and have suffered the most serious difficulties in earning a livelihood. In addition, most of the hibakusha who miraculously survived the nuclear hell, suffered the most serious mental shock and its after-effects. They have also suffered from discrimination in employment and marriage, and have prematurely aged. Their offspring, children and grandchildren, have never been free of the fear of genetic effects and the sudden onset of illness. For many hibakusha, the implications of life seemed then – and still seem – to have been lost. Most of them would say that they even envy those who died. There are several reports about the higher rate of hibakusha suicides. (In this meaning, nuclear omnicide includes delayed forced suicides also.) The human damage caused by the atomic bombing was not limited to the immediate postwar years. It has continued and expanded as time has passed. *It knows no limits of time or space.*[5]

Such problems of the hibakusha raise some new tasks of research for sociologists, such as the following: How can a sociological survey of the social, health and mental conditions of the hibakusha be made? Is it possible to make surveys in which attention is paid to the personal life history and spiritual history of the hibakusha? Naturally, such surveys have been impossible without the cooperation of the hibakusha themselves, and studies such as these were initiated by sociologists at Hiroshima University and later carried out by researchers in sociology, social policy, and social medicine at many universities, in cooperation with the hibakusha movement; the studies contributed very much to the appeal to the public concerning the serious damages suffered by hibakusha, thereby giving strength to the movements advocating both the denunciation of nuclear omnicide and the enactment of a "law for assistance and protection of hibakusha", although this is still ignored by the Japanese government.

3 Sociological implications of expanded genres of hibakusha

The damage suffered by citizens of Hiroshima and Nagasaki has not been limited to them alone. The first "damage" of the atomic bombing of Japan was totally unnecessary from the military and political standpoints. Japan was then at the point of surrender. Seen from the position of international law, it was a totally unjustifiable act of war and crime of genocide. The purposes were 1) to test the destructive power of atomic bombs on living human bodies, and 2) to initiate a blackmail policy against the Soviet Union[6] and other peoples. In this context, those two first atomic bombings had the inevitable result of starting the nuclear arms race which is currently under way. One year or perhaps just several months before the attack Drs. Niels Bohr, Leo Szilard, James Franck and other top level nuclear scientists, with deep insight into this inevitability, made desperate efforts to urge highly placed U.S. officials to refrain from using the bombs. Their efforts, however, were in vain.[7] As a result, humanity now stands in the position these men had foreseen. The nuclear omnicide of Hiroshima and Nagasaki gave impetus to the never-ending series of nuclear tests and the arms race, as well as the expansion of the nuclear fuel cycle, producing new genres of hibakusha all over the world. As I see it, the genres of hibakusha can be classified as follows:

I Hibakusha (Atomic Bombed)
a) Dead victims of Hiroshima and Nagasaki.
b) Living victims who survived the nuclear hell.
c) Hibakusha of the 2nd and 3rd generations.

II Hibakusha (Atomic Radiated)
a) U.S. and British soldiers who were ordered into Hiroshima and Nagasaki to dispose of nuclear waste, and later were found to be suffering atomic diseases.

b) Atomic citizens – Japanese fishermen as well as Pacific and American residents directly affected by the nuclear tests. There must also be such hibakusha in the Soviet Union, China and other nuclear power countries.

c) Atomic soldiers who participated in nuclear tests. In the U.S. the number of such hibakusha is estimated at somewhere between 250,000 and 500,000.[8] There must also be such hibakusha in the Soviet Union, China and other nuclear states.

d) Atomic workers exposed to radiation in the nuclear fuel cycle, which starts with uranium mining and continues with the refining of uranium and plutonium as well as manufacturing nuclear warheads and working in nuclear power plants, and in dealing with nuclear waste.[9]

e) Stillborn atomic babies who have died because of radioactive fallout from nuclear tests and plants.[10]

III Hibakusha (Atomic Threatened)

a) All human beings who have been forced to absorb into their bodies, more or less, the nuclear ashes of death produced and diffused by nuclear tests and the nuclear fuel cycle.

b) All human beings who have been and are threatened by nuclear blackmail and possible nuclear omnicide.

In summary, all members of human society are now hibakusha. Day and night, all are threatened with nuclear omnicide. It would be no exaggeration to say that all sociologists and all schools of sociology have never in their history faced such a great danger.

2 Sociological implications of the anti-nuclear weapons movement

1 Historical outline of the anti-nuclear weapons movement in Japan
In the context of the sociological implications of Hiroshima and Nagasaki as outlined above, we can well understand the social and historical background of the rise of the anti-nuclear weapons movement all over the world since around the year 1978, when the first Special Session on Disarmament (SSDI) of the UNO was held. History since Hiroshima and Nagasaki has witnessed the process of recognition of the significance of nuclear omnicide. In Japan, the

anti-nuclear weapons movement was initiated by surviving hibakusha who had experienced nuclear omnicide. They witnessed and documented that nuclear hell, defying the U.S. occupation forces, who refused to permit publication of any evidence or reports recorded by the hibakusha, threatening them with trial by a military tribunal and imprisonment. It was not until 1952 that the Japanese could openly publish documents setting out the facts without fear of suppression.

Since 1945 there have been five high tides of the anti-nuclear weapons movement in Japan, which I set out below:

1. 1950: Campaign in support of the "Stockholm Appeal" with some 6.450,000 signatures.

2. 1954-55: Massive protest meetings against U.S. nuclear tests at the Bikini Atoll in the Pacific as well as the first World Conference against the A & H Bombs and the formation of Gensuikyo (Japan Council against A & H Bombs) with 30.404,980 signatures of protest.

3. 1977-78: Temporary Unification of the anti-nuclear weapons movement and the campaign for anti-nuclear signatures, with 20.178,453 submitted to SSDI of the UNO.

4. 1982: Mass meeting in Tokyo, Hiroshima and other places as well as the campaign for anti-nuclear signatures totaling more than 29.000,000 on the occasion of SSDII.

5. 1985-86: Campaign for anti-nuclear signatures supporting "Appeal from Hiroshima and Nagasaki" with 20.486,534 signatures by the end of June 1986, as well as a campaign for nuclear-free declarations by local self-governing bodies. 1,023 of the total of 3,323 such communities had declared themselves "nuclear-free" by the end of June.

2 Sociological aspects of the anti-nuclear weapons movement

As the above shows, the anti-nuclear weapons movement has its own social and political background. With this as a precondition, it seems to me that the sociological implications of this movement can be outlined in the following way:

First, it is not a social movement that originates from immediate economic need and demand. In this sense, it is different from economic movements such as a labor movement for wage increases or employment.

Second, it is a political movement, but a political movement that does not represent the interests of any special political party or organization. The actors in it belong to all social groups, including hibakusha, workers, farmers, self-employed intellectuals, religionists, men and women, youth and aged, boys and girls, and even soldiers, officers, capitalists and monopoly capitalists, but not of course the nuclear military-industrial-complex and its supporters. It can also embrace all kinds of organizations: anti-nuclear organizations, political parties, trade unions, farmers' co-operatives, organizations of professionals, intellectuals, religionists, the youth and the aged, boys and girls, soldiers and officers, capitalists and even monopoly capitalists, *except* those of the nuclear military-industrial-complex and its accomplices. It is a most universal and supra-class political movement.

Third, it is a social movement to replace the old way of thinking among the people and their political leaders, with what Einstein called " a completely new way of thinking". In this sense, we can say that it is a cultural, ethical and philosophical movement of humankind who want to survive the most serious danger in human history. It cannot exist and function without the creation and diffusion of an anti-nuclear culture, nor without untiring efforts at anti-nuclear education. I would add that it is a social movement to appeal to common sense, reason, feeling and human imagination for survival.

Fourth, it cannot but be both national and international, because without national consensus and international agreement there can be no perspective for the abolition of nuclear weapons.

Fifth, it is a historical movement to resist any exterminist attempt to put an end to history itself. The task is urgent, but at this present time, there is no certainty that history will not be ended by nuclear omnicide. It will take many years for humankind to be completely free from this danger, and I fear that the task of the anti-nuclear weapons movement, that is, to ensure human survival, will not soon be accomplished.

Sixth, it is therefore expected that the anti-nuclear weapons movement must create the most massive, popular, enduring and varied forms. It seems that it is not by chance that in Japan the main forms of the movements have been the campaigns for collecting signatures to be submitted to self-governing communities, the government and the UN.

3 Sociological considerations on the campaigns for anti-nuclear signatures

As I have said, one of the high tides of the campaign for anti-nuclear signatures in Japan was from November 1977 through May 1978. On this campaign, Chifuren (National Federation of Local Ass'ns of Women) collected 5.323,352 signatures, 26,4% of the total of 20.178,453. in 1979, I made a sociological survey about how the local association of women organized the campaign at the level of the local community in Hiroshima city.[11]

Chifuren is considered to be the biggest independent and neutral women's organization in this country. We found that most of its grassroots leaders were conservative, and the campaign was mainly organized by women of influence in each neighborhood, and was reportedly encouraged by the mass media.

In contrast to the campaign in 1977-78, the campaign of 1985-86 has been independently initiated and organized by Gensuikyo, which is considered to be communist-oriented. This campaign has almost been ignored by other anti-nuclear organizations like the socialist-oriented Gensuikin as well as neutral organizations like Chifuren. (The political background to this might be explained by a change of policy of the Socialist Party, which, from 1980, signed an anti-communist agreement with the Komei Party.) The campaign has also been ignored by the mass media other than the organs of the Communist Party and Gensuikyo affiliated organizations.

The campaign was not a spontaneous move, but was purposefully organized. Gensuikyo set for itself the goal of collecting the signatures of half of the total population, nationally and locally. By the end of June 1986, the number of signatures collected amounted to 20.486,534, 34,3% of the target figure. It is noteworthy that such a number of signatures has never before been collected by only one anti-nuclear organization. At prefectural level, the highest rate (75,4% of half the population) has been accomplished in Kyoto Prefecture. The second (74,1%) in Wakayama Prefecture. At the level of cities, towns and villages, the highest rate (83,0% of the whole population) has been achieved in Kumanogawa town, Wakayama Prefecture and Chino city, Nagano Prefecture. I made a study of the local communities where the campaign has been organized. Their sociological and organizational aspects can be outlined as follows:

First, Gensuikyo and its branches at prefectural and local levels set up independent committees for the signature campaign, which were comprised of the leading personalities in trade unions, organizations of farmers, intellectuals, professionals, women and youth and other societies. The committees immediately asked men and women of influence, including a mayor or town headman, to endorse the campaign. It then sponsored and held many meetings showing anti-nuclear films or videos at the grassroots level. In this organizational work, members of trade unions affiliated with Toitsurousokon (communist-oriented Federation of Trade Unions for Promotion of a United Front) played a leading role.

Second, after such preparatory organizational work, each committee began the collection of signatures. The campaign was first organized *vertically* through the affiliated organizations of the committee. Then, committees for the campaign were set up by school districts, the smallest unit of a local community. Its leading personalities became activists in the campaign. In cooperation with them, activists of trade unions and other affiliated organizations were allotted some sections of each district. The campaign was then organized *horizontally,* and the day for united action was then decided. On this day, the activists, following the map of resident registration, visited every home, one by one. Some new ideas were created in order to achieve this goal. For example, a copy of the "Appeal from Hiroshima and Nagasaki" was delivered to each home the day before the united action day. By this means, the residents were given time to carefully read the text beforehand and discuss its implications with other members of the family. Families who happened to be away at the time were asked to make use of the copy by way of a folding letter addressed to the committee. Through such an expanded network of committees at various levels, the campaign was carried out *vertically* and *horizontally*.

Third, a decisive factor for the campaign was in asking leading personalities of local communities, especially a mayor, a headman of town or a village chief to become an endorser, which of course made it necessary for activists of the campaign to redouble their efforts to persuade them to become endorsers. But success in this endeavour gave the campaign prestige at grassroots levels, and made it easier to expand the organizational work. In many local communities, the administration itself provided the activists with the facilities of its own broadcasting system as well as public halls and other buildings. The signature campaign necessarily led to asking a local assembly to declare itself "nuclear free", a declaration that in return directly encouraged and promoted the signature campaign. In so far as the government of a local community abides by such a resolution, it cannot but play a politically and financially supportive role for the anti-nuclear signature campaign.

Fourth, Gensuikyo has its own staff of full time officers as well as its own office building. Most of its prefectural branches also have full time officers and offices. Without such a basis, it would have been impossible to conduct such a campaign, showing how important it is for the campaign to finance full-time officers and even to increase their number.

Fifth, for Gensuikyo and its branches to wage this campaign, it has always been necessary to organize a system of reciprocal communications, top to bottom and vice versa. To do this, it was necessary to equip the movement with a lot of electronic equipment, including computers, facsimile machines, Xerox, printers, word processors and so on. The process of the organization itself had to be planned and scheduled, and activists were expected to observe the scheduled plan and discipline.

It can be recalled in this connection that Lenin emphasized the necessity for the revolutionary movement to free itself of amateurishness and rebuild the organizational work on the principle of a great industry.[12] To me this thesis of Lenin still seems valid today for all kinds of democratic social movements, including the anti-nuclear weapons movement.

3 Toward a scientific theory of social movement

1 On theories of social movement

For many years, the social movement has been one of the most important subjects of sociology. The history of sociology could even be described as the history of theories of the social movement. One of the main trends in these theories might be called an irrationalist approach which stresses the emotional aspects of the mass and explains the social movement as a mob movement.[13] Another is the Marxist approach which understands social movements as forms of the class struggle, which is said to be finally explained by contradictions between productive forces and production relations. It is true that Marx, in *"Capital"*, made clear the economic laws of capitalist society and in this way made economics a science. His contributions cannot easily be overestimated.

However, can we say that the theory of social movement has already become a science even from a Marxist standpoint? Are there any sociological surveys of the real organizational conditions and process of social movements of political parties, trade unions, peace campaigns and so on from the point of view of Marxism? Certainly, there are many discussions about "what is to be done", but, as far as I know, very few about "what it is". First of all, sociological surveys should be conducted, and then, based on them, we would be able to make the theory of the social movement more scientific.

Another point which we should make clear is that theories of social movements as well as the sociologists behind them cannot take a so called "value free" or "neutrality" position regarding anti-nuclear weapons movements and related democratic social movements (anti-war and peace movements, municipal democratization movements, anti-pollution movements, etc.). This is so because the continuity and development of theories of social movements as well as the existence of researchers themselves are now being threatened by the possibility of nuclear war.

Without the success of anti-nuclear weapons movement and the consequent abolition of nuclear weapons, the survival of social movement theories and social scientists cannot be assured. How, then, can we be "value free" or "neutral" toward the anti-nuclear weapons movement in face of such a critical situation? Of course, our argumentation here does not intend to exclude critical studies on the *modus operandi* and organizational forms of the anti-nuclear weapons movement, but rather welcomes such critical studies. For the further development of the movement, it is desired that limitations and shortcomings of the anti-nuclear weapons movement should be first brought to light and then, at earliest possible time, be overcome.

2 Some theoretical theses

With the above thesis as my premise, I would like to suggest some theoretical theses,[14] which might be considered in our efforts to form a scientific theory of the social movement. In the first place, such a theory will have to include a theory of the development process of mass groups. Generally speaking, this process consists of three stages: a) a spontaneous un-organized and inner oriented group of a group *of itself* (an sich, to use Hegel's terminology), b) an organized but other-oriented group or a group *for itself* (für sich) and c) the most organized, self-oriented and independent group or a group *of and for itself* (an und für sich). Most mass groups forming a social movement for democratic goals develop themselves, starting from stage a), through stage b), to reach stage c). A leading group, already established as stage c), organizes and leads a stage a) group into stage b), and with the help of a group at stage b), seeks to organize the last into stage c). To do this, a leading group is always responsible to educate and raise the groups at the lower stages to the higher levels. A leading group can be such and expand its social movement only by being like a self-multiplying organism. Any democratic social movement can develop if it is organized and led by a leadership which always tries to *aufheben*, to use again Hegel's terminology, to raise itself.

Further, any social movement develops when such an organizational process goes from top to grassroots, and from national to local level. Perspectives through all vertical and horizontal levels should be provided. The conditions and demands of the people at grassroots are important. Any social movements, basing themselves solely on the grassroots level, can successfully develop. But this does not mean that the grassroots mass can consistently organize themselves and develop the social movement. They cannot acquire the proper perspective. Rather, the initiative, the approach and the perspective given by the leadership are the decisive points.

Moreover, this developmental process of groups is at the same time the process of the development of individual personalities which make up the groups. Individual personalities are not developed at stage a) Generally speaking, they are egocentric, apolitical and apathetic to most social and political problems. At stage b), they cannot help paying attention to the destiny of others, and become more or less organized and find it necessary to observe the principles of the group. At stage c), the members of the group seek to develop their individuality and to harmonize their individuality with the common interest of their group. They cannot but educate themselves to become all-round developed persons.

It seems to me that we can see such a process taking place in the anti-nuclear weapons movement in Japan, especially in areas where the signature campaign has been successfully organized. The urgent task of the abolition of nuclear weapons surely requires such a process to be further developed and accelerated.

Finally, I would like to emphasize the point that the development of the anti-nuclear weapons movement is the process of developing the democratic systematization of the masses, both horizontally and vertically, and further both extensively and intensively. Anti-nuclear weapon movement is in two meanings the biggest and the most thorough-going democratic movement in the history of mankind. For one thing, it is a mass movement to isolate the most undemocratic and autocratic nuclear powers to play on extermination of humankind. On the other hand, the overwhelming majority of the masses must organize themselves in the most democratic way in order to insure the success of anti-nuclear weapons movement. In other words, only the total development of democracy can fulfill the aims of anti-nuclear weapons movement.

3 Concluding remarks

The history of the anti-nuclear weapons movement is long and the scope of the movement is extremely far-reaching. Although I do realize the difficulties in doing research on the anti-nuclear movement, I do not hesitate to say that such research ought to be carried out both individually and in groups by as many researchers as possible. I am of the opinion that the movement can be further developed by clarification of social law of its development and theorization of the practice. It would be no exaggeration to say that every school of sociology needs to study the sociological and organizational aspects of the anti-nuclear weapons movement, thereby contributing to the survival of society and humankind, including sociologists and their schools. I hope that this short article provides tentative assumption to promote the further development of the anti-nuclear weapons movement as well as the study on it.[15]

Notes

1) A Call from Hibakusha of Hiroshima and Nagasaki: Proceedings of International Symposium on Damage and After-Effects of Atomic Bombing of Hiroshima and Nagasaki, Asahi Evening News, Tokyo 1978; the Committee for Compilation of Materials in Damage caused by Atomic Bombs in *Hiroshima and Nagasaki, Hiroshima and Nagasaki: The Physical, Medical and Social Effects of the Atomic Bombing,* Basic Books, New York, 1981.

2) S. Shibata: *Lessons of the Vietnam War,* Grüner, Amsterdam, 1973.

3) Ibid., especially Chapter II "The Vietnam War and the Tasks of Social Science".

4) J. Somerville: *Philosophy and Ethics in the Nuclear Age,* Japanese version, Tokyo, 1980; "Nuclear 'War' Is Omnicide" in *Nuclear War,* ed. by M.A Fox and L. Groarke, Peter Lang, New York, 1985.

5) See books cited in note 1).

6) G. Alperovitz: *Atomic Diplomacy*, Simon & Schuster, New York, 1985, enlarged new edition.

7) M.J. Sherwin: *A World Destroyed,* A.A. Knopf, New York, 1973.

8) H.L. Rosenberg: *Atomic Soldiers,* Beacon Press, Boston 1980; L.J. Freeman: *Nuclear Witnesses,* N.Y. 1981; T.H. Saffer and W.S. Kelly: *Countdown Zero,* New York, 1982 and H. Wasserman and others: *Killing Our Own,* New York, 1982.

9) See the books cited in note 8).

10) E.J. Sternglass: *Low-level Radiation,* N.Y. 1972; H. Caldicott: *Nuclear Madness,* Brookline, 1978.

11) S. Shibata and K. Kimoto: "Sociological Study of the Movement for Prohibition of Nuclear Weaponry" in *Yearbook of Social Scientific Studies,* No 6, in Japanese, Tokyo, 1982.

12) V.I Lenin: W*hat is to be done?,* 1902.

13) For example, see G. Le Bon: *Psychologie des foules,* 1895; K. Young: *Handbook of Social Psychology,* London, 1946.

14) My organizational theory of the social movement is described in detail in my book *Theory of Human Nature and Personality*, in Japanese, Tokyo, 1961. I was helped significantly by the works of A. Gramsci and A.S. Makarenko.

15) The article is based on the paper presented at the eleventh world congress of sociology, New Delhi, India, August 18-22, 1986 as well as 'hankakuundou no shakaiundouronteki kousatsu', in *Kagaku to Shisou,* No.62, 1986.

The Peace Movements for the Future – From a Survey on Swedish Peace Movements

Katsuya Kodama
Lund University Peace Research Institute

1 The new wave of peace movements

The big swell in new peace movements at the end of 1970s and in the beginning of 1980s was a political event which had a significant impact on many citizens' way of thinking about peace and security issues. In response to NATOs double track decision to deploy Pershing IIs and cruise missiles, large peace movements arose in many of the West-European countries. The mass demonstrations and gatherings in opposition to nuclear weapons held in several large cities of western Europe are still fresh in our memory. The wave quickly crossed the Atlantic to the United States, where the freeze resolution and funding for new weapons systems became the main issues. Stimulated by these movements, Japan also experienced both the emergence of new peace movements and the revival of previously existing peace movements. These movements in Japan attempted to issue a warning to the government that it must maintain its three previously established non-nuclear policies (policies prohibiting production, possession or deployment of any nuclear weapons on Japanese soil). In addition, it is important to mention several attempts to establish new independent peace groups which are not affiliated with official government organizations in some of the East-European countries.

Some peace organizations and initiatives, such as the Green party in West-Germany, No to Nuclear Weapons in Denmark and Norway, and the Freeze campaign, were newly born. At the same time, some old peace organizations, such as CND (Campaign for Nuclear Disarmament) in the United Kingdom and the Peace and Arbitration Society in Sweden were revitalized and renewed to meet the demands of the present age. The wave of these popular movements, with some unique characteristics different from the previous ones, are called the new peace movements. Although many of these movements have been less active during the last few years, the impact of these activities should not be underestimated.

This surprising wave has obviously created new research interest in peace movements among sociologists in Western Europe. However, in spite of some significant contributions by Frank Parkin (1968), Johan Galtung (1964), Anders Boserup and Claus Iversen (1966) and others, it may be safe to say that the peace movement had been an study area curiously neglected by sociologists until very recently.

Since the beginning of 1970s, a number of theorists of 'new social movements' have emerged. Among those associated with this tradition are, for example, Alain Touraine, Jean Cohen, Claus Offe, Hanspeter Kriesi, Klaus Eder and Jürgen Habermas. In the beginning, they concentrated their attention on the women's movements and the environmentalist movements. As the new wave of peace movements spread in the West-European countries, however, they began to direct more attention toward peace movements as a means of establishing a theoretical framework for 'new social movements'. In fact, more sophisticated and substantial argumentation regarding 'new social movements' has become possible in 1980s, because new peace movements have provided fresh inspiration and new theoretical ground for such social movement theories.

This tradition of 'new social movements' theory will soon be established in the context of the theory of social movements. Despite the increasing consolidation and sophistication of the theory, however, a significant amount of ambiguity and confusion remain, partly due to the lack of empirical data for further research. One of the goals of the present paper is to clarify and develop the theory by providing more empirical data on social backgrounds, attitudes, political opinions, manner of thinking and values of peace activists. Our extensive survey of members of peace organizations in Sweden attempts to focus on features of current peace movements and to propose a new paradigm for peace movements. By so doing, we hope to be able to discover the implications of peace movements for the society of the future.

2 Method

In order to meet our research goals, an extensive questionnaire survey was undertaken from November, 1988 to February, 1989. The following is a brief description of the method used in that survey.[1]

a) Selection of Target Organizations
Each peace organization has its own specificities. In fact, some researchers have specifically noted diversification and heterogenity as one of the important characteristics of the new peace movements. Therefore, the selection of target organizations must be made in light of this new dynamic. Five criteria have been used for selection. First, an organization should have peace, or some aspect of it, as their sole or predominant goal. This excludes a number of political, religious, labor, social and other organizations where peace is but one programme point among several.

Second, an organization should offer individual membership. This excludes a number of organizations, such as *Svenska fredsrådet* (the Swedish Peace Council). Third, an organization should be focused, even if not necessarily exclusively, on negative peace in Galtung's sense, that is the absence of war and similar forms of violence, and the absence of preparations for such activities. Fourth, they should have a substantial number of members. They should be large and active enough to be visible to and recognized by the public, not just by a small group. Finally, they should encompass a broad spectrum of citizens. Recently, a number of occupational organizations for peace, such as the Physicians against Nuclear Weapons and Engineers for Peace have appeared, but they have been not been included in the survey.

The above criteria have led to the selection of the following organizations; the Swedish Peace and Arbitration Society (SPAS), the Christian Peace Movement, the Swedish Peace Committee, the Swedish section of Women's International League for Peace and Freedom (WILPF) and Women for Peace. In addition to these organizations, sampling was also taken from the general public, for comparative purposes.

b) Sampling

Since we were not allowed to obtain a copy of the membership list, the survey was done under our guidance by the staff of each organization. The points which they were instructed to follow were: 1) to select *completely randomly* 300 members out of the total membership; 2) to avoid organizations, groups and families on the member list from sampling; 3) to select members living in Sweden and avoid members living in other Scandinavian countries or other foreign countries; 4) to include all the individual members - both those affiliated directly with the central organization and those affiliated with the local branch or other groups - in the selection process.

Our survey of the general public was undertaken differently. The Swedish telephone directories were used for this. The survey was administered in the following way; 1) the number of samples were allocated according to the size of the telephone directory in each area; 2) female and male names were selected alternately so that the number of each gender would be equal; 3) otherwise the 300 individual names and addresses were chosen completely at random.

c) Return Ratio

Given the nature of the cooperation from peace organizations, the number of answers from our samples of peace organizations is higher than we expected. The return ratio from the samples of the Peace Committee is low because reminders were not sent to them because of technical difficulties. The return ratio from the survey of the general public is also comparatively low, but if one takes into consideration the recent trend toward increasing scepticism over questionnaire surveys among the general public, the figure is acceptable. The following table shows the return ratio from the samples of each group. Because of address changes and mortality, a number of the envelopes were returned unopened. Therefore, the number of subjects reached by the mail survey is slightly lower than 300 for each group.

Table 1 Return ratio

Group	sending-1	reminder-1	reminder-2	return ratio
Christian Peace M.	185 (63%)	40 (14%)	32 (11%)	257/295 (87%)
Peace Committee	134 (45%)	-	-	134/297 (45%)
SPAS	179 (60%)	66 (22%)	19 (6%)	264/296 (89%)
WILPF	185 (63%)	37 (13%)	30 (10%)	252/296 (85%)
Women for Peace	154 (52%)	33 (11%)	37 (13%)	224/295 (76%)
General Public	111 (41%)	30 (11%)	28 (10%)	169/270 (63%)
Sum	948 (54%)	206 (12%)	146 (8%)	1300/1749 (74%)

The first questionnaire was sent for the first time in November, 1988. The first reminder was sent in December, 1988 and the second reminder in February, 1989.

3 Profiles of the target organizations

A number of scholars and activists have already published their works on the history and organizational frameworks of Swedish peace movements (e.g. Andersson & Lindkvist, 1985; Nordland & Elster, 1983; Lassinantti, 1983; Lindkvist, 1989). It is not our main aim to provide an historical and organizational analysis of Swedish peace movements. However, to facilitate better understanding and analysis of the data from the questionnaire survey, it is of considerable merit to briefly profile the target organizations.

a) The Christian Peace Movement

This organization has its roots in the Swedish World Peace Mission (*Svenska världsfredsmissionen*), founded in 1919, and the Association for Christian Society (*Förbundet för kristet samhällsliv*), founded in 1918. The radical pacifist sections of the two organizations merged in 1969 and the present name has been used since 1977. It is now Sweden's second largest peace organization with a membership of 4,000. It publishes the bimonthly magazine, *Fred & Framtid*. The Christian Peace Movement promotes the realization of justice and peace from a Christian perspective. Its programme is extensive and includes many issues ranging from the Nordic nuclear-free zone and nuclear power plants, to North-South issues.

b) The Peace Committee

This organization was founded in 1949 and grew rapidly in connection with the so-called Stockholm Appeal against nuclear weapons issued in 1950. It is regarded as 'an anti-imperialist front organization for peace and in support of liberation movements against fascism and oppression'. The Peace Committee has some 2,000 individual members and several Swedish interest organizations are also affiliated with it. It publishes the magazine, *Fred & Solidaritet*. It is a Swedish member organization of the World Council in which the official East-European Peace Committees predominate.

c) The SPAS (Swedish Peace and Arbitration Society)

SPAS, founded in 1888, is the world's oldest peace organization existing today and Sweden's largest peace organization with a membership of 15,000. The organizational structure of the SPAS is highly decentralized. There are around 120 local societies which plan their own activities such as studies, debates, demonstrations, meetings, non-violent actions, *etc.*, while the board of directors and a central office with 13 employees are located in Stockholm. SPAS publishes a monthly newspaper, *PAX*, which has a circulation of 18,000. SPAS's current campaigns include support for a Nordic nuclear-free zone, a Comprehensive Nuclear Test Ban Treaty as well as opposition to nuclear weapons and Swedish weapons exports.

d) The Women's International League for Peace and Freedom (Swedish section)

WILPF was founded in 1915 and the Swedish section was established four years later. The membership of Swedish section is around 2,000. This organization is distinguished by its very extensive international cooperation with sister organizations throughout the world. The International League has consultative status in UNESCO, ECOSOC, FAO, ILO and UNCTAD. The Swedish section became a promoting organization of "the Great Peace Journey" in 1984 and 1985, which successfully drew world attention. *Fred och Frihet* is published from the Swedish section.

e) Women for Peace

Women for peace is a very new peace group, which was founded in 1978 and formalized in 1981. Women for Peace become known because it took the initiative, together with its equally recently started Nordic sister organizations, in organizing the peace marches of Nordic women to Paris in 1981, to Moscow and Minsk in 1982, and to New York and Washington in 1983. It has a grass-roots character and its structure is extremely decentralized. Although it has central office in Stockholm, central control and coordination are kept to a minimum level. Every local group decides its own activities, such as study circles, demonstrations, public meetings and peace manifestation arrangements. At hay season, it had a membership of nearly 3,000 which at present is cut by approximately a half. It publishes the bimonthly magazine, *Kvinnor för Fred*.

4 Activists

a) Well-Educated Middle Class?

A few studies on the class backgrounds of peace activists are available for our discussion of the peace movements of the 1960s. Frank Parkin's study of the Campaign for Nuclear Disarmament (CND) in the United Kingdom showed that the members of the movement were mainly drawn from highly educated people of the middle class (Parkin, 1968). Herman Schmid, in his study of Swedish Peace and Arbitration Society, also demonstrated the concentration of the well-educated middle classes among the activists (Schmid, 1966).

A number of scholars on peace movements have also argued that the core of the new peace movements consists of the well-educated middle classes, although they seem to lack concrete proof for their conclusions (e.g. Salomon, 1986). However, opinion polls conducted in Britain, Italy, the Netherlands, Norway, the Federal Republic of Germany and the United States in 1982 support their arguments. These polls indicate that anxiety about nuclear weapons is most prevalent among the well-educated middle classes (International Herald Tribune, October 10, 1982). Although strong anxiety about nuclear weapons among the well-educated middle classes does not unequivocally demonstrate their frequent participation in peace movements, the data can be used as supportive evidence for the argument.

Theorists of "new social movements" are largely in line with this argument, but their discussions seem to be slightly more sophisticated. Claus Offe (1985) argues that the new social movements consist of "three rather sharply circumscribed segments of the social structure, namely 1) the new middle class, especially those elements of it which work in the human service professions and/or the public sector, 2) elements of the old middle class, and 3) a category of the population consisting of people outside the labor market or in a peripheral position to it (such as unemployed workers, students, housewives, retired persons, etc.)".

Hanspeter Kriesi's research (1989) gives us some concrete data on the social backgrounds of "sympathizers" in new social movements. Kriesi analyzed the data from the Dutch national election survey of 1986. His analysis demonstrates that, "although the Dutch new social movements are supported by broad segments of the population, their inner circles are predominantly constituted by segments of the reconceptualized new class: the young specialists in social and cultural services, and some of the young administrative specialists in public service". He also mentioned that a particularly high level of support for the new social movement comes from the young, the highly educated, the unemployed, women and students.

Some sociological works recently carried out by the British Campaign for Nuclear Disarmament also give us fresh insights on the class background of activists. Peter Nias (1983) made surveys of CND's national membership, of marchers attending the CND 1982 National Demonstration in London, and of the European Nuclear Disarmament (END) movement's membership. According to Nias's survey on CND membership, less than 10 % of those sampled had manual or unskilled jobs while more than 50 % held managerial or professional occupations. Surveys on END emphasized the trend. 70 % of the sample held professional employment with less than 5 % participation from manual and unskilled workers. Paul Byrne's similar survey (1988) also shows that 63 % of the membership was from the middle-class occupations. John Mattausch (1986) conducted semi-structured tape-recorded interviews with randomly selected samples of activists and lay-members drawn from two local CND groups sited in markedly different towns. From the result of the research, he argues that "CND is best seen as individuals employed predominantly in one part of the state, the welfare dimension, protesting against the threat emanating from the warfare dimension of the state" (Mattausch, 1989).

We will first examine the educational dimension. Table 2 clearly shows the very high level of education of peace activists. The educational level of members of the Peace Committee is relatively low, but even that is higher than the level of the general public. There is no doubt that the peace activists are highly educated.

Table 2 Educational level

Group	primary	secondary	univ.student	univ.degree	A.V.
Christian Peace M.	11%	28%	12%	48%	(1,97)
Peace Committee	35%	27%	5%	34%	(1,37)
SPAS	16%	35%	4%	43%	(1,77)
WILPF	13%	29%	4%	53%	(1,97)
Women for Peace	17%	25%	6%	52%	(1,93)
General Public	40%	38%	1%	21%	(1,02)

[A.V.(Average Value); 0 value was given to those who graduated from only compulsory school, and 1 to those from secondary school, 2 to university students and 3 to those who have a university degree. Average Value shows roughly the level of education of each group.]

Our questionnaire contained two questions on occupational position and sector which are identical to the ones used in previous surveys (Schmid, 1966; Halle, 1966; Galtung, 1964; etc.). The results are shown in Table 3 and Table 4. First, let's examine Table 3. Students are over-represented in the membership of peace organizations in comparison with the general public. It is probable that due to the use of the telephone directory for sampling of the general public, our samples appear to include slightly less students than the national population statistics would indicate. The number of full time university students is around 223 000, which is 3% of the whole population (Year Book of Nordic Statistics, 1985). Even compared to this figure, students are over-represented, especially in the Christian Peace Movement, the Peace Committee and SPAS.

It is obvious that workers and laborers are under-represented, while office employees are highly over-represented in peace movements. It is noteworthy that the Peace Committee has more laborers and less office employees than the other four peace organizations. In spite of the over-representation of white collar workers, those who hold executive positions are slightly less numerous in peace organizations than in the general public. This clearly shows that peace activists are occupationally centered in middle class.

In spite of the commonly held assertion, we don't find an over-representation of housewives and unemployed persons in memberships of peace movements. With the exception of the Christian Peace Movement, pensioners are over-represented in the samples of peace organizations, compared with the general public.

Table 3 Occupational positions

	A	B	C	D	E	F	G	H	N.A.
Christian Peace M.	12%	12%	46%	12%	7%	4%	0%	4%	3%
	(30)	(30)	(119)	(32)	(18)	(9)	(1)	(11)	(7)
Peace Committee	7%	22%	38%	4%	7%	2%	1%	11%	6%
	(10)	(29)	(51)	(6)	(10)	(3)	(2)	(15)	(8)
SPAS	10%	12%	42%	8%	8%	1%	2%	13%	5%
	(27)	(31)	(110)	(22)	(20)	(2)	(4)	(35)	(13)
WILPF	3%	6%	48%	7%	10%	3%	1%	19%	3%
	(7)	(15)	(120)	(18)	(26)	(8)	(2)	(48)	(8)
Women for Peace	3%	6%	42%	14%	13%	3%	1%	13%	6%
	(7)	(14)	(93)	(31)	(29)	(6)	(3)	(28)	(13)
General Public	1%	27%	29%	14%	10%	4%	2%	7%	5%
	(2)	(45)	(49)	(24)	(17)	(7)	(4)	(12)	(9)

A) student, apprentices
B) worker, laborer
C) office employee, white collar
D) leading position
E) independent position (free occupation, owner of business enterprise, etc.)
F) housewife
G) unemployment
H) pensioner

Table 4 Occupational sector

	A	B	C	D	E	F	G	H	N.A.
Christian Peace M.	4%	11%	3%	5%	49%	4%	0%	4%	19%
	(9)	(29)	(8)	(14)	(125)	(10)	(1)	(11)	(50)
Peace Committee	1%	17%	4%	10%	34%	1%	1%	11%	19%
	(1)	(23)	(5)	(14)	(45)	(2)	(2)	(15)	(26)
SPAS	2%	9%	3%	6%	41%	2%	2%	13%	22%
	(6)	(24)	(9)	(16)	(109)	(4)	(4)	(35)	(57)
WILPF	2%	2%	3%	3%	51%	4%	1%	19%	15%
	(4)	(6)	(8)	(8)	(129)	(9)	(2)	(48)	(38)
Women for Peace	1%	6%	2%	7%	51%	4%	1%	13%	16%
	(2)	(13)	(5)	(16)	(114)	(8)	(3)	(28)	(35)
General Public	5%	20%	14%	10%	27%	5%	2%	7%	10%
	(8)	(34)	(24)	(17)	(45)	(8)	(4)	(12)	(17)
General Public*	5%	29%	14%	14%	34%	2%	3%	-----	-----

A) agriculture, forestry, fishery
B) industry, mining, craft
C) trade, restaurant, hotel
D) communication, transport, post, telephone-telegraph
E) public administration
F) domestic works
G) unemployment
H) pensioner

(General Public* shows the data at the end of 1984 from Yearbook of Nordic Statistics 1985.)

Table 4 also gives us interesting data. We find an apparent under-representation of those who engage in primary and secondary sectors. The differences between samples of the peace organizations and the general public are especially conspicuous. The Peace Committee again constitutes an exception here, and the difference with the general public is very small. As already mentioned above, this may be the result of the participation of members of labour movements in the Peace Committee.

There are big differences in the tertiary sector, depending on the manner in which types of occupations are specified. There are proportionally fewer people in peace organizations than the general public who engage in such occupations as trade, restaurant and craft as well as communication, transport, post and telephone-telegraph. On the contrary, those in public administration are highly over-represented. This is especially noted in the two women's organizations and the Christian Peace Movement, which constitute around half of all the samples.

From our examination of Table 2, 3 and 4, we conclude that peace activists are highly educated members of the middle class with white collar occupation. Those with state employment occupation are especially over-represented among peace activists. The category of people with marginal occupations or without solid occupation (e.g. students and the retired) are also over-represented among the activists. Multi-variate analysis could develop our findings in more sophisticated ways, but we are prevented from presenting a complicated analysis by the present limitation of space.[2]

5 Post-materialist values

Through his extensive survey, Ronald Inglehart (1971 & 1977) ascertained that a "silent revolution" in values and attitudes had occurred among the public of some West-European countries. By "silent revolution", he means the shift of values of the public from an overwhelming emphasis on material well-being and physical security toward greater emphasis on the quality of life. Concerning political skills, Inglehart ascertains that an increasingly large proportion of the public is going to have sufficient interest and understanding of national and international politics to participate in decision-making at this level. According to him, current changes enable the mass publics to play an increasingly active role in formulating policy, and to engage in what might be called 'elite-challenging' as opposed to 'elite-directed' activities. One of his main findings is that the age cohorts who had experienced the wars and scarcities of the era preceding the rapid economic rehabilitation and further development in Europe accord a relatively high priority to economic security and security needs. On the contrary, the younger cohorts possess a set of "post-bourgeois" values which relate to the need for belonging and to esthetic and intellectual issues.

Sociologists on "new social movements" have argued that such changes in values and attitudes are markedly noticed among participants of social movements. One of the leading theorists in this field, Alain Touraine argues that social movements are much more than mass protests against the state. The emergence of a new generation of social movements indicates the transition from industrial capitalist society to programmed civil society, in which a set of post-materialist, or post-materialist values constitute key concepts. He examines the self-understanding and ideologies of contemporary movements and focuses on cultural issues of the movements, regarding the creation of new identity and norms (Touraine, 1981).

Another leading sociologist, Jean L. Cohen also discusses cultural aspects of post-industrial society. According to Cohen, post-industrial society is an allegedly new societal type characterized by new focuses of power, forms of domination, modes of investment, and a "reflexive" cultural model. Power, investment, and domination are located at the level of cultural production. Cohen further argues that the developments to post-industrial society governs the change in the identity of collective actions and the kinds of movements they develop. Therefore, for Cohen, "the struggle for the democratization of society, and the concern with participatory forms of association on the part of contemporary collective actors, are due to recognition that not only the means but also the ends of social production are social products". (Cohen, 1985)

Jürgen Habermas (1981) similarly maintains that the new conflicts arise in areas of cultural reproduction, social integration, and socialization. The question which social movements address to is, according to Habermas, not one of compensations that the welfare state can provide, but rather how to defend or reinstate endangered life styles, or how to put reformed life styles into practice. In short, he contends that the new conflicts are not sparked by *problems of distribution*, but concern the *grammar of forms of life*. According to him, these new politics, which post-materialist values are closely connected with and find support in the new middle class, the younger generation, and those groups with higher levels of formal education.

More specifically on peace movements, Kim Salomon (1986) argues that the peace movements are essentially *anti-establishment* movements, with post-material values whose central concepts are participation, solidarity and self-determination. The new peace movements are not merely opposed to nuclear weapons, but also to entire cultures and value systems which exhibit strong links with nuclear weapons. In the new peace movements, Salomon maintains, nuclear weapons are considered symbolic of authoritarian, materialistic, bureaucratic, and male-dominated culture.

In this regard, women's (peace) movements and ecologists' (peace) movements merit special attention. According to the perspective of women's movements, nuclear weapons and war systems are the products of authoritarian male culture, and therefore, the whole value system must be changed in order to get rid of the nuclear weapons. They go so far as to say that we should stop discussing national security issues in terms of numbers of guns, because such a discussion reinforces the militaristic-materialistic culture, without questioning its fatal assumptions (cf. Pietilä, 1984). Ecologists' peace movements and the Green party in West-Germany, for example, are also strong critics of 'industrial' values. They do not accept the traditional concept of progress and criticize the established authorities. We must note that there are some differences and disagreements concerning the extent of this trend inside the groups. Despite the differences, however, the basic characteristics of the movement can easily be acknowledged. The fact that 'Green' representatives wear T-shirts at their Congress seems to have a symbolic implication. They are not only ecologists and peace activists, but also the resistants to the established authority and creators of the new society of post-industrial culture (cf. Bahro, 1986).

A number of researchers have reported that the new peace movements are informal, *ad hoc*, egalitarian and participation-oriented. The freeze campaign in the United States (Lewis, 1984), the Green party in West-Germany (Wehr, 1986), No to Nuclear Weapons in Norway (Grepstad, 1981) and No to Nuclear Weapons in Denmark (Krasner & Petersen, 1986) are reported as highly informal and decentralized. A group which is perhaps symbolic of this point is the group of Women camping outside the Greenham Common military base. Although they have existed for a number of years, they have not developed a formal, systematized organizational structure. They have neither formal membership, nor formal leadership. Spontaneous participation of individuals is a fundamental principle of their operation. This grass-roots character of the new peace movements is a logical necessity of the post-industrial culture.

a) Data Analysis

One important problem is how to measure the possession of post-materialist values. In 1970 and in 1971, the European Community carried out public opinion surveys in France, West Germany, Belgium, the Netherlands, and Italy. Data for 1970 are also available from Great Britain. These surveys included a series of questions designed to indicate which values an individual would rank highest when forced to choose between security or "materialist" values such as economic and political stability; and expressive or "post-materialist" values. Ronald Inglehart (1971 & 1977) utilized the questions for identifying the extent of these post-materialist, or post-industrial values. The question was as follows;

"If you had to choose among the following things, which are the two that seem most desirable to you?"
     __ Maintaining order in the nation
     __ Giving the people more say in important political decision
     __ Fighting rising prices
     __ Protecting freedom of speech

According to Inglehart, emphasis on order (first answer) and economic stability (third answer) can be termed a materialist set of value priorities, while choice of the items concerning political participation (second answer) or free speech (fourth answer) reflects emphasis on post-materialist values. On the basis of the choices made among these four items, Inglehart classified respondents into basically three value-priority types, namely a pure materialist type (order and economic stability), a pure post-materialist type (political participation and free speech) and a type in between (other mixed choices).

We have followed Inglehart and used the same question for our analysis. To facilitate data analysis, we assigned values to the three value-priority types. The value 2 is assigned to a pure post-materialist type, 1 to a type in between and 0 to a pure materialist type. First, we will examine average values of post-materialist, or post-industrialist orientation of our six groups.

Table 5 Post-material orientation of peace organizations

Groups	materialist	in-between	post-mater.	N.A	average v.
Christian Peace M.	1 (0%)	91 (35%)	163 (63%)	2 (1%)	1,64
Peace Committee	1 (1%)	41 (31%)	91 (68%)	1 (1%)	1,68
SPAS	3 (1%)	83 (31%)	176 (67%)	2 (1%)	1,66
WILPF	6 (2%)	91 (36%)	151 (60%)	4 (2%)	1,58
Women for Peace	2 (1%)	52 (23%)	169 (75%)	1 (0%)	1,75
General Public	20 (12%)	112 (66%)	34 (20%)	3 (2%)	1,08

The contrast between peace activists and the general public is striking. Approximately two thirds of peace activists of all the five organizations have a post-material orientation, compared to only one in five among the general public. Obviously, there are much larger proportion of post-materialists in the peace movements than in the general public. The differences among the five peace organizations are very small. We note, however, that Women for Peace has slightly more post-materialists than other peace organizations, but the difference is not so salient.

We will also examine the relation between the level of peace activism and the possession of post-material values. Table 6 shows the average value index along the level of peace activism.

Table 6 Level of peace activism and post-material values

Groups / activism	low	middle	high	correlation
Christian Peace M.	1,50	1,67	1,81	+,18
Peace Committee	1,20	1,75	1,72	+,23
SPAS	1,51	1,70	1,68	+,08
WILPF	1,34	1,59	1,67	+,16
Women for Peace	1,17	1,82	1,80	+,20
General Public	0,99	1,57	1,50	+,31

We can easily see *the general trend that the more one is involved in peace movements, the stronger post-materialist values one possesses.* Correlation coefficients between the level of activism and possession of post-materialist values are positive and meaningful. But we find that in the Peace Committee, SPAS, Women for Peace and General Public, middle level activists have slightly higher indexes than the high level activists. This provides us with the very interesting hypothesis that core activists may hold more strongly materialist values than the rank and file. However, this can not be proven at present because the differences in the value index are very small and the two other peace organizations don't show a parallel trend. A larger scale survey which allows for more detailed analysis is surely needed in order to examine this new hypothesis.

Through the examination of Table 5 and Table 6, it seems quite possible and sufficient here to say that peace activists possess post-materialist values more strongly than the general public.

6 Political ideology

The basic ideology cherished by the peace movements of the past, – e.g. the uprising in 1950s-60s and anti-Vietnam war movements – is a mixture of anti-imperialism and (nuclear) pacifism. Most of those involved in these movements criticized the American government and other allied powers for their imperialistic entanglement in the build-up of nuclear weapons or the Vietnam war. Many of those who protested in this manner belonged to the *'Marxist'* or *'new left'* political culture and values, although we should not neglect to mention some important exceptions such as apolitical radicals and religious pacifists. Some earlier movements even argued that the Soviet Union is a power acting on behalf of peace against American imperialism and that Soviet nuclear missiles are of a purely defensive character.

Political culture and values in the new peace movements are rather different. The heated nuclear arms race between the two blocks has cast a certain amount of doubt upon the belief in the 'peaceful character of Soviet missiles' as well as the validity of the notion of balance of power. The new peace movements do not accept the concept of *defensive* nuclear weapons. They argue that, *any nuclear weapons, regardless of which political bloc possesses them, are offensive and perilous.* The new movements make a harsh charge not only against the deployment of American nuclear missiles, but also against the deployment of Soviet nuclear missiles, e.g. the SS-20. It is not an exaggeration to say that nuclear pacifism is a key political ideology in the new peace movements.

Another important element, which is closely connected with what we have argued above, is that the activists attempt to go beyond the bloc theory. The East-West problem and how abolish the bloc system are dominant topics of discussion in the new peace movements. The theory of a balance of power, which is still advocated by military strategists and some politicians, is extremely unpopular among the new peace movements. This theory is, in fact, the frequent target of criticism. What the new peace movements in Europe are attempting to do is to create a unified and non-nuclear "greater Europe", by transcending the notion of bloc confrontation.

On this point, the special attention given by the West-European peace movements to the independent peace movements of Eastern Europe is worthy of attention. Since the beginning of the 1980´s, a few attempts to establish unofficial, or independent peace groups in the Eastern bloc have been reported. They are, for example, the 'Moscow Trust Group' in USSR, the 'Peace Group for Dialogue' in Hungary, and the 'Church Peace Movements' in GDR. These movements have been heartily welcomed by many of the Western peace movements. In fact, these attempts have been well covered by the magazines of West-European peace movements, e.g. *Journal of European Nuclear Disarmament.*

One question which must be asked is: "Why are peace groups in the West paying so much attention to the small groups in the Eastern bloc when doing so might risk jeopardizing relations with the much bigger official peace movements there?" The answer is to be found in their belief in bringing about de-nuclearization *by transcending the bloc system.* What the new peace movements are seeking is not merely détente between the two blocs but a new world order without antagonism between the two blocs. Their belief is that a dialogue with official movements which are so closely related the government in Moscow will not contribute to transcending the bloc system and might even consolidate it, even though it has some potential to promote détente between the two divided blocs. The existence of independent peace movements is considered to be crucial by the West European movements. Without such movements, they believe that it is not possible to move beyond block theory and its model of the world. They seek co-operation with unofficial groups in the opposite political bloc which will not only call for de-nuclearization but also question the authoritative control by Moscow. If there is no such group to be found, they try to persuade people to establish such groups. The new peace movements are so passionately concerned about independent peace movements in the Eastern bloc, because the issue touches upon their central belief that the world order itself must be changed before their goals have a chance of being fully realized.

a) Data Analysis
Our questionnaire contains a few questions to tap U.S.– Soviet orientation. The Table 7, 8 and 9 show the responses to these questions.

Table 7 Responsibility for political tension

Question A; Which country do you think has the main responsibility for the political tension in the world today?

Groups / answer	U.S.A.	Soviet Union	more or less same	N.A.
Christian Peace M.	13%(33)	0%(1)	84%(215)	3%(8)
Peace Committee	82%(110)	0%(0)	14%(19)	4%(5)
SPAS	24%(62)	1%(2)	75%(197)	1%(3)
WILPF	15%(37)	1%(3)	83%(208)	2%(4)
Women for Peace	25%(57)	0%(1)	73%(163)	1%(3)
General Public	4% (7)	11% (19)	82%(139)	2%(4)

From Table 7 we can easily see that the majority of respondents answered that the U.S.A. and the Soviet Union share the responsibility for the political tension in the world. As many as 70 to 90% of the respondents from both peace organizations and the general public expressed the view that the responsibility of the U.S.A. and the Soviet Union is more or less same, with the Peace Committee as the only exception. The majority of respondents from the Peace Committee answered that the U.S.A. is more responsible than the Soviet Union for tension in the world. This is not so surprising, because 'the Peace Committee is an anti-imperialistic front organization for peace, for support of liberation movements against fascism and oppression', as the programme of the organization states. To criticize the imperialistic militarism of the United States is a natural consequence of this approach. If we compare the general public with the other four peace organizations, the general public assigns more responsibility to the Soviet Union (11%) than to the U.S.A.(4%), while respondents of the four peace organizations place more responsibility on the shoulders of the U.S.A.(13-25%) than on the Soviet Union (0-1%). There are differences between peace organizations and the general public in this respect, but it seems to be more important that the vast majority of not only the general public but also of peace activists of the four organizations asserted that the U.S.A. and the Soviet Union are more less equally responsible for world tensions.

Table 8 Soviet Union as a military threat

Question B; Do you see the military forces of the Soviet Union as a threat against us?

Groups/answer	yes	probably	no	don't know	N.A.
Christian Peace M.	34%(87)	37%(94)	25%(64)	4%(11)	0%(1)
Peace Committee	7%(9)	9%(12)	82%(110)	1%(1)	1%(2)
SPAS	29%(76)	33%(88)	25%(64)	4%(10)	0%(0)
WILPF	31%(80)	34%(85)	27%(68)	6%(14)	2%(4)
Women for Peace	38%(84)	26%(59)	34%(75)	2%(4)	0%(1)
General Public	34%(57)	31%(52)	27%(45)	8%(13)	1%(2)

Table 9 U.S. as a military threat

Question C; Do you see the military forces of the United States as a threat against us?

Groups/answer	yes	probably	no	don't know	N.A.
Christian Peace M.	33%(84)	30%(76)	33%(84)	5%(12)	0%(1)
Peace Committee	52%(69)	26%(35)	20%(27)	1%(1)	1%(2)

SPAS	35%(91)	31%(82)	30%(78)	5%(13)	0%(0)
WILPF	33%(82)	33%(83)	28%(70)	5%(12)	1%(3)
Women for Peace	50%(112)	26%(59)	19%(43)	4%(8)	0%(1)
General Public	11%(19)	22%(37)	55%(93)	11%(18)	1%(2)

Except for the Peace Committee, the proportion of answers to a question regarding the Soviet Union as a military threat and regarding the U.S.A as military threat are very similar among the respondents. Approximately one third answered 'yes' to both questions B and C, and more or less same the respondents answered 'probably' to both questions and one third answered 'no'. In other words, the number of respondents who see the military forces of the Soviet Union as a threat is almost same as those who see the military forces of the U.S.A. as a threat, among the Christian Peace Movement, SPAS, WILPF and Women for Peace. In order to make clear the relations between question B and C, we here show correlation coefficients. An answer of 'yes' was coded by 2, 'probably' by 1, and 'no' with a value of 0 for both questions.

Table 10 Correlations between question B and question C

Groups	correlation coefficients
Christian Peace Movement	+0,68
Peace Committee	+0,09
SPAS	+0,68
WILPF	+0,58
Women for Peace	+0,55
General Public	+0,44

The correlation coefficients between question B and C are very high among the peace organizations, with the exception of the Peace Committee. The correlation coefficient among the general public is also high, but slightly lower than those of the four peace organizations. It is clear, especially among peace activists of the four organizations, that many of those who see the military forces of the Soviet Union as a threat also see the military forces of the U.S.A. as a threat. At the same time, many of those who don't see the Soviet Union as threat think that the American military is not a threat.

Our findings from the examinations of Table 7, 8, 9 and 10 are compatible with the argument that the new peace movements criticize both the superpowers for their possession of offensive nuclear weapons and that they attempt to bring about de-nuclearization by transcending the bloc system. The exception of the Peace Committee can be explained by their anti-imperialistic character which results in a somewhat different approach to this issue.

7 Environmentalism

According to Oberschall (1973), a worldwide ecological movement started in the United States in the 1950s as a citizens' movement against the pollution of the environment. Spontaneous protests were initially provoked by local events and subsequently environmental protection groups were formed in population centers in the United States.

It is not until 1960s, however, that the general public acquired a high level of environmental consciousness. Cramer, Eyerman and Jamison (1987) distinguish three phases of the rise of environmental consciousness. The first phase (1962-1968), can be characterized as one of public and individual education concerning environmental issues. The second period (1969-1973) was obviously the heyday of environmental concern in most of the industrially developed countries. A lot of media campaigns and demonstrations against environmental pollution were organized during this period. The third phase 1974-1986 was, in the opinion of the authors, a period of the fragmentation of knowledge interests.

During the second phase 1969-1973, ecological movements were very successful in mobilization and drew marked attention not only from the general public but also from sociologists. It is during this period that theorists of new social movements, such as Touraine, began to develop their ideas. For such analysts, the environmental movements, together with feminism became one of the most important models for new social movements. It is interesting to note that the period 1974-1986, when knowledge interests of environmental issues were fragmented turns out to be an extremely successful period for peace movements. A number of scholars have already noticed that newly mobilized peace movements took over not only the cultural style and *modus operandi* but even the membership of environmental movements.

It is not just a coincidence that the Green party, which started as an ecology movement, has become one of the leading peace organizations not just in West-Germany but in the whole world. Their "alternative policy" or "alternative idea" (Bahro, 1986; Die Grünen, 1983) is a central doctrine relating to both ecological issues and peace issues. The Green party is made up of such new social movements as the ecology, anti-nuclear power, nuclear pacifism, anti-militarism and youth movements. What interests us is that there is a kind of conformity or fusion of these topics. Joachim Hirsch (1982) notes on West German peace movement in which Green party plays a leading role as follows;

> "The fight of the ecology movement is directed both against 'peaceful' atomic plants and missile bases. Its criticism of the independent large-scale technology takes into account the armament dynamics from which it surely cannot be separated. The connection between the form of the metropolitan growth of the economy and the military oppression of the Third World is at least tendentially reflected and, last but not least, the connection between the militarization of society and the oppression of women is fully recognized."

These coalitions, or even fusions of social movements are not confined to movements in West Germany but have been recognized in many other West-European countries. Environmental/ ecological/ green movements in the West share some "new" features, compatible goals and membership with women's, peace, and community movements (Frank & Fuentes, 1988). This is why a number of sociologists classify these movements together under the rubric of new social movements. Interaction and fusion of peace movements, environmentalism, feminism, etc., is one of the important characteristics of these new social movements.

We can assume that when international tension between the West and the East increases, the core of new social movements will direct their attention to peace issues and mobilize the masses for peace movements. When the tension slackens (at least in the eyes of general public) and environment concerns are raised because of some events like accidents at nuclear power plants, the core of new social movements change the focus of attention from peace issues to environmental issues. In such a case, environmental movements will be revitalized, while peace movements will lose vitality. In fact, during the late 1980s, peace movements have obviously lost their momentum, while environmental movements have been re-vitalized partly because of accident of Chernobyl nuclear power plant and the huge death toll of North Sea seals caused by a virus but nevertheless complicated by pollution. It is important to note that this approach assumes that the peace movements and environmental movements are so well integrated and related that they replace each other under certain circumstances.

If this assumption is correct, peace activists will register a high level of concern about environmental problems, and green activists will exhibit a high level of interest in peace issues. If this were not the case, quick and smooth transformations of movements could not occur. In the following, we will seek to examine this issue by reference to our data from the questionnaire survey.

a) Data Analysis
Our questionnaire contains the following four questions specifically about environmental issues. Tables 11, 12, 13 and 14 show the answers of these questions.

Table 11 Demonstration against nuclear energy

Question A) Here is an item which is occasionally the object of demonstrations. Would you consider participating in [demonstrations against nuclear energy]?

A) yes__;   B) no__;   C) have already participated__;

Groups/answers	yes	no	participated	N.A.	A.V.
Christian Peace M.	50%(129)	17%(43)	26%(68)	7%(17)	1,10
Peace Committee	21%(28)	31%(42)	37%(49)	11%(15)	1,06
SPAS	37%(98)	14%(37)	39%(104)	9%(25)	1,28
WILPF	31%(78)	14%(35)	46%(115)	10%(24)	1,35
Women for Peace	28%(62)	4%(8)	66%(148)	3%(6)	1,64
General Public	22%(38)	56%(94)	8%(13)	14%(24)	0,44

A.V. means the average of these values. A.V. answers of 'have already participated' were coded by value 2, 'yes' by value 1 and 'no' by value 0.

Table 12 Opinion about government's proposal on nuclear plants

B) The government has proposed that the phasing-out of nuclear power plants will be started by the middle of 1990s, when two reactors are to be closed down. Do you think that the government's proposal to the phasing-out of nuclear plants means that the process of phasing-out is going too fast or too slow or in good pace, or do you think nuclear power should not be terminated?

A) too slow__;   B) in good pace__;   C) too fast__;   D) should not be terminated__;

Answers	A	B	C	D	N.A.	A.V.
C.P.M.	45%(115)	47%(121)	3%(7)	4%(10)	2%(4)	2,35
Peace Com.	35%(47)	25%(33)	19%(13)	30%(40)	1%(1)	1,65
SPAS	50%(131)	43%(113)	4%(10)	2%(6)	2%(4)	2,42
WILPF	50%(123)	42%(107)	7%(18)	0%(1)	1%(3)	2,41
Women f. P.	66%(148)	32%(71)	1%(3)	0%(0)	1%(2)	2,65
Public	18%(31)	37%(63)	15%(25)	28%(48)	1%(2)	1,46

A.V. means the average of these values. Answer A was coded by value 3, answer B by value 2, answer C by value 1 and answer D by value 0.

The difference between the two questions is that question A includes the participation dimension, while question B seeks only to elicit opinion. However, it seems safe to say that both question A and B tap the problem of nuclear power plants. In fact, correlation coefficients between the two questions are in most cases very high (Christian Peace Movement +0,43; Peace Committee +0,75; SPAS. +0,47; WILPF +0,39; Women for Peace +0,20; General Public +0,59). The orders of average values from question A and B are almost the same. The average values for the general public are the lowest among the six groups for both questions and the average values for the Peace Committee are the second lowest. The Christian Peace Movement has the third lowest average values, while Women for Peace has the highest and SPAS and WILPF also have high average values on both questions. Obviously, there are significant differences among peace organizations in the degree to which they support the anti-nuclear power movement. In spite of the differences, however, it is safe and sufficient here to say that peace activists are more critical of nuclear power than the general public.

Table 13 Speed limit on motorway

C) Do you think that the speed limit should be lowered on our motorway or 110-highway for the sake of the environment?

A) not to be lowered   B) to be lowered by 10 km/h.   C) to be lowered by 20 km/h.

Groups/answers	A) not	B) by 10 km.	C) by 20 km	N.A.	A.V.
Christian Peace M.	19%(48)	30%(77)	51%(130)	1%(2)	1,32
Peace Committee	20%(27)	30%(40)	47%(63)	3%(4)	1,28
SPAS	8%(21)	25%(66)	65%(172)	2%(5)	1,53
WILPF	5%(13)	27%(69)	65%(164)	2%(6)	1,61
Women for Peace	7%(16)	21%(46)	71%(158)	2%(4)	1,65
General Public	44%(75)	17%(29)	36%(61)	2%(4)	0,92

A.V. means the average of these values. Answer A was coded by value 0, answer B by value 1, and answer C by value 2.

Table 14 Food without pesticides

D) Are you willing to pay more for food if you know that it is produced without pesticides or not? You are prepared to pay;

A) much more   B) a little bit more   C) not willing to pay more   D) don't know

Groups/answers	much more	a bit more	not more	D.K./N.A.	A.V.
Christian Peace M.	31%(79)	62%(159)	3%(7)	5%(12)	1,28
Peace Committee	23%(31)	49%(65)	19%(26)	9%(12)	1,04
SPAS	38%(99)	55%(146)	5%(12)	3%(7)	1,33

WILPF	50%(127)	44%(112)	2%(5)	3%(8)	1,49
Women for Peace	44%(98)	51%(114)	4%(10)	1%(2)	1,39
General Public	22%(38)	53%(89)	17%(28)	8%(14)	1,06

A.V. means the average of these values. Answer A was coded by value 2, answer B by value 1, and answer C by value 0.

The orders of the average values in Table 13 and 14 are almost the same as those of Table 11 and 12. SPAS, WILPF and Women for Peace have very high marks, while the average values of the general public are among the lowest levels on both tables. The Peace Committee has the lowest average values on both tables among peace organizations, and especially on Table 14, it is even slightly lower than that of the general public. We assume that this is at least partly due to the characteristics of traditional social movements, labour movements, which the Peace Committee is said to possess.

From the examination on Table 11, 12, 13 and 14, we can easily confirm our hypothesis that, in general, peace activists have more serious concerns about environmental issues and are therefore more supportive of environmental movement than the general public. The Peace Committee seems to be more concerned about other issues than the other peace organizations, but still tends to be more concerned than the general public.

8 Feminism

It has been argued, that "one of the most thoroughly sustained" findings of the social sciences, is that men are more likely to participate in politics than women (Milbrath, 1981). Theorists of "new social movements", however, have claimed that this does not apply to today's political movements with new characteristics, including peace movements. It should be noted that the new peace movements are surprisingly dominated by women. While the role of women in earlier peace movements was by no means insignificant, it was not as important as it is in the new movements. Despite the continuous existence of the Women's International for Peace and Freedom (WILPF) since 1915, the continuity of a broad women's anti-militarist tradition only became clear in the late 1970s with their independent role in the new peace movements (Young, 1983).

On 12 December, 1982, some tens of thousands of women from the United Kingdom and continental Europe surrounded the air base at Greenham Common, where cruise missiles were to be deployed. It is well-known that a small group of women have camped outside the base for years despite occasional imprisonment. In like manner, the idea of a women's peace camp has spread to other military bases in England, as well as to the Netherlands, Sicily, Canada and the United States.

Women in the Scandinavian countries have also been active. A group of women from Norway submitted a proposal to march from Copenhagen to Paris in 1981. Women for Peace groups, in support of the march, sprung up all over Scandinavia and 6 000 women (along with 4 000 men) participated in the march. This was followed by a massive peace rally in Gothenburg, Sweden in May 1982. These marches developed into 'The Great Peace Journey' activities.

The past decade has witnessed the appearance of some outstanding female peace activists and researchers, such as Alva Myrdal, Helen Caldicott and Petra Kelly. Most of them have consciously advocated feminist views on peace by noting a relation between peace and sexual equality. They do not hesitate to say that women can and must play a crucial role in creating world peace, because women, being brought up as the more peaceful gender, are more capable of solving conflicts in a non-violent way than men. It is important to note here that feminists do not merely oppose weapon systems, but also the male-oriented authoritarian culture which is, in their eyes, the root causes of such weapons systems. They emphasize the importance of equality, solidarity, love and spontaneity, while authority, order, control and bureaucratization are targeted for criticism. Their plan is to establish a new paradigm for peace movements and peace research. In this regard, it is important that female peace researchers have different priorities for their research agenda than male researchers (Boulding, 1983; Brock-Utne, 1985). They argue that there is too much (mindless) weapon counting in peace research and too little about cultural aspects of our society which relate to the issues of peace and war.

Our hypotheses here are that peace activists are supportive of women's liberation and that women are playing important roles in peace movements because they tend to adopt more pacifist opinions and attitudes. Our questionnaire contained a question on women's liberation. Table 15 profiles the response to this question.

Table 15 Peace movements and women's liberation

Question A) Here is an item which is occasionally the object of demonstrations. Would you consider participating in? < women's liberation >

A) yes__;   B) no__;   C) have already participated__;

Groups/answers		yes	no	participated	N.A.	A.V.
C.P.M.	F.	(34)	(49)	(8)	(29)	0,55
	M.	(40)	(56)	(3)	(35)	0,46
	total	29%(74)	41%(106)	4%(11)	26%(66)	0,50
Peace Com.	F.	(14)	(6)	(17)	(8)	1,30
	M.	(38)	(12)	(13)	(22)	1,02
	total	40%(53)	13%(18)	23%(31)	24%(32)	1,13
SPAS	F.	(61)	(33)	(24)	(34)	0,92
	M.	(39)	(39)	(8)	(23)	0,64
	total	40%(100)	27%(72)	13%(33)	22%(59)	0,81
WILPF	F.	(80)	(47)	(78)	(41)	1,48
	M.	(0)	(0)	(0)	(0)	---
	total	33%(84)	19%(47)	31%(78)	17%(43)	1,15
Women f.P.	F.	(70)	(22)	(103)	(28)	1,42
	M.	(1)	(0)	(0)	(0)	---
	total	32%(71)	10%(22)	46%(103)	13%(28)	1,41
Public	F.	(20)	(35)	(4)	(22)	0,47
	M.	(5)	(55)	(0)	(23)	0,08
	total	15%(25)	55%(93)	2%(4)	28%(47)	0,27

A.V. means the average of the values. Answers of 'have already participated' were coded by value 2, 'yes' by value 1 and 'no' by value 0.

100

The two women's peace organizations naturally have very high average values. The Peace Committee and SPAS also have rather high average values, which demonstrate their strong support for women's liberation. The Christian Peace Movement has the lowest average value among peace organizations, but even this is much higher than that of the general public. Thus it is a simple matter to draw the conclusion that peace activists are favorable toward women's liberation, in comparison with the general public. Another point which attracts our attention is that the differences in average values between men and women are smaller in peace movements than in the general public. Nearly all male respondents of the general public answered 'no' to the question A, while around one third of male respondents of the Christian Peace Movement and SPAS as well as nearly half of male respondents of the Peace Committee answered 'yes'. Not many men have already participated in demonstrations for women's liberation, but a substantial number of men expressed their willingness to participate. Our data indicate that male peace activists have strongly sympathetic attitudes and opinions about feminism.

We will now seek to establish whether or not there is a gender difference related to pacifist orientation. Table 16 and 17 show the results of question E and F respectively.

Table 16 Sweden and disarmament

Question E) How do you think Sweden should act concerning disarmament?

A) Sweden should disarm even if no other countries disarm.
B) Sweden should disarm if our neighbor countries disarm
C) Sweden should disarm only if all other countries disarm
D) don't know

Groups/answers		A)	B)	C)	D.K./N.A.	A.V.
C.P.M.	F.	(79)	(9)	(13)	(19)	1,65
	M.	(95)	(17)	(10)	(12)	1,70
	total	68%(176)	10%(26)	9%(24)	12%(31)	1,67
Peace Com.	F.	(36)	(3)	(2)	(4)	1,83
	M.	(67)	(9)	(6)	(3)	1,74
	total	80%(107)	9%(12)	6%(8)	4%(6)	1,78
SPAS	F.	(99)	(21)	(13)	(19)	1,65
	M.	(79)	(10)	(12)	(8)	1,66
	total	68%(180)	12%(32)	9%(25)	10%(27)	1,65
WILPF	F.	(114)	(36)	(66)	(34)	1,22
	M.	(1)	(1)	(0)	(0)	---
	total	46%(115)	15%(37)	26%(66)	13%(34)	1,22
Women f.P.	F.	(127)	(28)	(24)	(44)	1,56
	M.	(1)	(0)	(0)	(0)	---
	total	57%(128)	13%(28)	11%(24)	20%(44)	1,58
Public	F.	(14)	(6)	(34)	(27)	0,63
	M.	(13)	(17)	(45)	(8)	0,57
	total	16%(27)	14%(24)	49%(83)	21%(35)	0,58

A.V. means the average of these values. Answers A was coded by value 2, answer B by value 1 and answer C by 0.

Table 17 Armed resistance against attack

Question F) Suppose Sweden is attacked. Do you think we should offer armed resistance, even if the results appears uncertain to us?

A) yes__: B) no__: C) don't know__:

Groups/answers		yes	no	D.K./N.A.	A.V.
Christian Peace.M.	F.	(23)	(51)	(46)	1,24
	M.	(22)	(79)	(33)	1,44
	total	18%(45)	51%(132)	31%(80)	1,35
Peace Committee	F.	(17)	(14)	(14)	0,93
	M.	(49)	(19)	(17)	0,63
	total	51%(68)	25%(33)	25%(33)	0,72
SPAS	F.	(37)	(65)	(50)	1,19
	M.	(31)	(56)	(22)	1,23
	total	26%(69)	46%(122)	33%(73)	1,21
WILPF	F.	(94)	(73)	(83)	0,91
	M.	(1)	(0)	(1)	---
	total	38%(95)	29%(73)	33%(84)	0,91
Women for Peace	F.	(69)	(70)	(84)	1,05
	M.	(0)	(0)	(1)	---
	total	31%(69)	31%(70)	38%(85)	1,00
General Public	F.	(48)	(6)	(27)	0,45
	M.	(66)	(6)	(11)	0,26
	total	69%(116)	8%(13)	24%(40)	0,36

A.V. means the average of these values. Answers of 'no' were coded by value 2, 'yes' by value 0 and 'don't know' by 0.

A number of public opinion surveys have already demonstrated that women are more concerned about peace and war issues than men. Our data confirm this trend. In both Table 16 and 17, women have slightly higher average values than men in the general public. Thus among the general public, it seems safe to say that women have a more pacifist orientation than men. This finding is consistent with the argumentation of some female peace researchers and activists that women, being brought up as the more peaceful gender, are more inclined to solving conflicts in a non-violent way than men.

When we examine the opinions of the peace activists themselves, however, differences between the two genders are not that clear. In the Christian Peace Movement, men seem to be slightly more pacifist in orientation than women, while the trend in the Peace Committee is totally the reverse. There are almost no differences between male and female samples of SPAS. There are two possible explanations. One explanation is that other factors might be more important variables for measuring the impact of pacifist orientation of peace activists than gender. The other explanation is that male peace activists are, so to say, *feminized* in this respect. In fact, unilateral disarmament (question E) and giving up armed resistance (question F) are both traditionally considered to be expressions of weakness and feminity. It could be that feminism has already had a strong impact not only on female peace activists but also on male activists. We can assume that the differences between the two genders on pacifist orientation become less clear among peace activists, because male activists are *feminized* and have adopted a way of thinking similar to that of female activists. Our findings in Table 15 show that male peace activists have favorable attitudes to feminism support this reasoning.We are not sure which explanation is the most accurate, but the notion of the feminization of male activists offers some interesting possibilities.

9 Concluding remarks

A few years have already passed since the surprisingly heated and large wave of peace movements in the beginning of 1980s. Now a number of peace researchers, political scientists and sociologists have begun to evaluate the effects – negative and positive – of the last wave of peace movements. One of our concerns with the arguments used in these discussions is that many of them tend to see peace movements only as pressure groups or political movements on peace and conflict issues. They tend to argue the success and failure of peace movements only on the basis of real changes in policy making. When U.S. nuclear missiles were deployed in Europe, some declared the complete defeat of peace movements and criticized peace movements for their incompetence. In their eyes, peace movements are no more than political pressure groups, and peace movements are simply meaningless if they fail to give visible impact on national or international policy-making.

What we have attempted to show in this article is that peace movements are more than mere political pressure groups which simply demand policy changes on military issues. Peace movements challenge not only a government's policy on military issues but also call into question social structures, ways of thinking, life styles, values, *etc*. The society they are pursuing might be called the post-materialist society, civil society, green society, post-industrial society, alternative society or feminist society. Although their visions may not be clearly formulated yet, it can safely be argued that peace movements challenge the present male-authoritarian militaristic society and attempt to transform it into a society in which equality, environmentalism, solidarity, self-determination and peace are the basic principles. The extent to which such a society has been realized is, in my view, one of the most important indicators of success or failure of peace movements.

Notes

1) I would like to express my sincere gratitude for kind cooperation of many peace activists and the Swedish peace organizations to the questionnaire survey. I do hope that findings from the survey will, in one way or another, be useful for peace activists who participated in the project, too.

2) Multi-variate analysis has confirmed that the core actors of peace movements are the educated middle classes *with one or two socially handicapped conditions*. Because we lack the space for such complicated analysis, we do not go into details here. I hope to publish the results later.

References

Andersson, Jan & Lindkvist, Kent :"The Peace Movement in Sweden", in Kalterfleiter, Werner & Pfaltzgraff, Robert L. (eds.):*The Peace Movements in Europe and the United States*, Croom Heim, London & Sydney 1985.

Bahro, Rudolf:*Building the Green Movement*, GMP Publishers Ltd, London, 1986.

Bell, Daniel: "The New Class; A Muddled Concept", in Bruce-Briggs,B. (ed.):*The New Class?* Transaction, New Brunswick, N.J, 1979.

Boserup, Anders & Iversen, Claus: "Demonstrations as a Source of Change; A Study of British and Danish Easter March", in *Journal of Peace Research*, Vol.3, No.4, 1966.

Boulding, Elise:"Peace Movement in U.S.A.", in *International Peace Research Newsletter*, Vol.XXI, No. 3, 1983.

Brock-Utne, Birgit: *Educating for Peace; A Feminist Perspective*, Pergamon Press, New York, 1985.

Byrne, Paul: *The Campaign for Nuclear Disarmament*, Croom Helm, London, New York & Sydney, 1988.

Cohen, Jean: "Rethinking Social Movements", in *Berkeley Journal of Sociology*, Vol.XXVII, 1983.

Cohen, Jean: "Strategy or Identity; New Theoretical Paradigms and Contemporary Social Movements", in *Social Research*, Vol. 52, No. 4, 1985.

Cramer, Eyerman & Jamison: "The Knowledge Interests of the Environmental Movement and Its Potential for Influencing the Development of Science", in *The Social Direction of Public Sciences; Sociology of Sciences Yearbook XI,* 1987.

Die Grünen:*Programme of the German Green Party*, GMP Publishers Ltd, London, 1983.

Frank & Fuentes:"Ten Theses on Social Movements", (unpublished paper), 1988.

Galtung, Johan: "Foreign Policy Opinion as a Function of Social Position", in *Journal of Peace Research*, Vol. 1, No. 3-4, 1964.

Grepstad, Jon :"Norway and the Struggle for Nuclear Disarmament", a paper prepared for 1981 World Conference Against Atomic and Hydrogen Bombs. Tokyo, Hiroshima & Nagasaki, 1981.

Habermas, Jürgen:"New Social Movement", in *Telos*, 49, Fall, 1981.

Habermas, Jürgen: "Historical Consciousness and Post-Traditional Identity; Remarks on the Federal Republic's Orientation to the West", *Acta Sociologica*, 31, 1988.

Halle, N.: "Social Position and Foreign Policy Attitudes", in *Journal of Peace Research*, No. 1, 1966.

Heberle, Rudolf: *Social Movement; An Introduction to Political Sociology*, Appleton-Century-Crofts, New York, 1951.

Inglehart, Ronald: "The Silent Revolution in Europe; Intergenerational Change in Post-Industrial Society", in *The American Political Science Review*, Vol. 65, 1971.

Inglehart, Ronald: *The Silent Revolution; Changing Values and Political Styles among Western Publics*, Princeton University Press, Princeton. N.J, 1977.

Isernia, Pierangelo: "Public Opinion and Peace Mobilization", A Paper Presented at the XIth General Conference of IPRA. Sussex, U.K, 1986.

Hirsch, Joachim: "The West German Peace Movement", in *Telos* 51, Spring, 1982.

Krasner, M. & Petersen, N.:"Peace and Politics; Danish Peace Movement and Its Impact on National Security Policy", in *Journal of Peace Research*, Vol. 23, No. 2, 1986.

Krasner, Michael: "Decline and Persistence in the Contemporary Danish and British Peace Movements; A Comparative Analysis", in Kodama, K. & Vesa, U. (eds.):*Towards a Comparative Analysis of Peace Movements*, Dartmouth Publishing Company, U.K. (in print) 1989.

Kriesi, Hanspeter: "New Social Movements and the New Class in the Netherlands", in *AJS* Vol. 94 No. 5, 1989.

Lassinantti, Gunnar*Current Sweden – The Peace Movements in Sweden*, The Swedish Institute, Stockholm, 1983.

Lewis, David: "Tough Choices for the Freeze", in *Not Man Apart*, October, 1984.

Lindkvist, Kent:"Mobilization Peaks and Declines of the Swedish Peace Movement", in Kodama, K. & Vesa, U. (eds.):*Towards a Comparative Analysis of Peace Movements*, Dartmouth Publishing Company, U.K. (in print) 1989.

Mattausch, John: "The Sociology of CND", in Creeighton, C. & Shaw, M. (eds.): *The Sociology of War and Peace*, Macmillan Press, London, 1987.

Mattausch, John: *A Commitment to Campaign; A Sociological Study of CND*, Manchester University Press, Manchester & New York, 1989.

Milbrath, Lester W.: "Political Participation", in The Handbook of Political Behavior; Vol. 4, Long, S.L. (ed.) Plenum, New York, 1981.

Nias, Peter: "The Poverty of Peace Protest", unpublished MA thesis, Postgraduate School of Studies in Peace Studies, University of Bradford, 1983.

Nordland & Elster: *Fredsrötter; En Handbok i Fredsarbete*, Wahlström & Widstrand, Stockholm, 1983.

Offe, Claus:"New Social Movements; Challenging the Boundaries of Institutional Politics", in *Social Research*, Winter 1985.

Overschall, Anthony: *Social Conflict and Social Movements*, Prentice Hall, Englewood Cliffs, N.J., 1973.

Parkin, Frank: *Middle Class Radicalism; The Social Bases of the British Campaign for Nuclear Disarmament*, Manchester University, Manchester, 1968.

Pietilä, Hilka:"Women's Peace Movement as an Innovative Proponent of the Peace Movement as a Whole", in *IFDA Dossier*, 43, September 1984.

Salomon, Kim: "The Peace Movement – an Anti-Establishment Movement", in *Journal of Peace Research*, Vol. 23, No. 2, 1986.

Schmid, Herman: "On a Study of a Swedish Peace Organization", A Paper Presented at the Second Nordic Conference on Peace Research, Hilleröd, Denmark, 1966.

Touraine, Alain: *The Voice and the Eye; An Analysis of Social Movements*, Cambridge University Press, 1981.

Wehr, Paul: "Disarmament Movements in the United States", *Journal of Peace Research*, Vol. 23, No. 2, 1986.

Young, Nigel:"The Contemporary European Anti-Nuclear Movement", as; *PRIO Working Paper* 3, 1983.

Trident Town: Action-Research and the Peace Movement

Paul Smoker
Richardson Institute for Peace Studies
Lancaster University

Introduction

Barrow in Furness on the British Cumbrian coast houses the Vickers submarine construction complex. It is here that work on the Trident submarine project began in the early 1980s. Trident submarines if they are deployed in the early 1990s will represent a significant upgrading in the UKs current naval strategic nuclear force, the Polaris fleet of nuclear powered nuclear armed submarines.

The British Peace Movement has campaigned consistently against the deployment of Trident, a deployment they see as a major escalation in both qualitative and quantitative aspects of the British nuclear deterrent. This paper describes the course of an action-research project involving Barrow in Furness Campaign for Nuclear Disarmament (CND) and the Richardson Institute for Peace Studies, Lancaster University.

The action-research involved in the project was perhaps unique for the British Peace Movement as it involved a preliminary survey that was used to guide a subsequent year long peace action campaign in Barrow. A second survey was then undertaken one year after the first in order to evaluate the possible effectiveness of the peace action campaign in Barrow with regard to attitudes towards Trident.

This paper describes the initial survey in 1985, the peace action campaign undertaken by Barrow CND during 1985 and 1986, and the results of the follow up survey taken in 1986. It concludes with some comments on the value of this type of action research project.

2 The 1985 survey

On Saturday May 18th 1985 a survey was conducted in Barrow between the hours of 10.00 a.m. and 1.00 p.m.. A total of 561 people were interviewed by fifteen interviewers placed at 7 locations. The survey had been pretested and was designed to be administered relatively quickly in public places such as shopping centres, public libraries, parks, bus stops and car parks. The interviewers all had a basic training and were clearly identified as being associated with a research unit at Lancaster University.

The sample comprised 52% men and 48% women, the age and sex break down of the sample was

	- 20	20-30	30-40	40-50	50-60	- 60
Male	6%	13%	11%	8%	6%	6%
Female	6%	11%	12%	5%	4%	5%
Total	13%	25%	23%	14%	10%	12%

(Sub totals do not always add up to totals due to rounding figures up and down to whole number percentages.)

The survey asked 13 questions, and before considering cross tabulations the general results are summarised as follows.

i. Simple percentages
(1) Do you think Trident is necessary for the defence of this country?

	Yes	No	Don't know
	50%	36%	12%

National surveys at that time recorded a 50% plus rejection of Trident, but it is of some interest that even in "Trident Town" Barrow, where the shipyard is by far the largest employer, just half the population at that time viewed Trident as necessary for the defence of the country.

(2) Is the fire power of Trident

Less than Polaris	*1%*	*About the same as Polaris*	*5%*
Greater than Polaris	*58%*	*Don't know*	*34%*

Most people knew or guessed that Trident was more powerful than Polaris, although 34% answered Don't know.

(3) Do you think that building Trident at Barrow makes the future of Vickers

Less secure	*13%*	*Stable*	*27%*
More secure	*51%*	*Don't know*	*8%*

About half of those interviewed felt that the building of Trident made the future of Vickers shipyard more secure, while only 13% felt building Trident made Vicker's future less secure.

(4) How many Trident submarines are to be built at Barrow?

1	*4*	*8*	*16*	*Don't know*
2%	*27%*	*9%*	*2%*	*57%*

About one quarter of the sample knew that 4 Trident submarines were to be built, most people didn't know.

(5) Would you prefer Vickers to build something rather than Trident?

Yes	*No*	*Don't know*
69%	*18%*	*13%*

There was a clear preference for alternative production at Vickers. In fact the Bradford School of Peace Studies project on alternative production for Vickers began at about this time.

(6) The estimated cost of Trident is (in millions of pounds £M)

£1M	£10M	£100M	£1,000M	£10,000M	Don't know
0	8%	10%	13%	25%	42%

Again one quarter of the sample knew the cost of the Trident or simply picked the highest figure.

(7) Do you think this expenditure on Trident is justified?

Yes	No	Don't know
35%	49%	14%

About one third think the expenditure on Trident is justified, while about one half feel it is not justified. Taken with items 1 and 5 it is clear that in Barrow Trident was accepted as a "necessary but undesirable evil"

(8) What percentage of this cost will be spent in the United States?

None	About 20%	About 50%	About 70%	Don't know
1%	10%	22%	16%	49%

Less than one quarter knew or guessed the correct answer of 50%. Taken with the other knowledge items this further illustrates the lack of knowledge about Trident.

(9) Put in order of preference what the Governments spending priorities should be. (The answers are best illustrated with reference to percentage support for the top two preferences)

	Priority 1	Priority 2
Health Service	63%	26%
Education	20%	44%
Military Expenditure	5%	5%
Social Services	10%	21%

Health and education are understandably seen as priorities, but the connections between expenditure on Trident and cuts elsewhere may not be properly realised.

(10) What do the initials C.N.D. stand for? (The answers are best illustrated by classifying them right or wrong. Thus "the peace movement" or "nuclear disarmament" are coded as right.)

Right	Wrong
64%	36%

Roughly two thirds of those asked knew, in a general way at least, what C.N.D. stood for.

(11) Do you think that Barrow and District C.N.D. has made you more aware of nuclear weapons and the Trident programme?

Yes	No	Don't know
42%	49%	8%

By mid 1985 about half the sample said they had not been made more aware of nuclear weapons and the Trident programme by Barrow CND.

(12) Do you support C.N.D.?	*Yes*	*No*	*Don't know*
	29%	55%	14%

Most people in Barrow do not support CND, the distribution of 29% and 55% being close to but probably less favourable to CND than what was probably the national average. For example a national poll undertaken by Marplan gave the following results.

Marplan Question: Britain is safer having its own nuclear weapons.

	1984	*1985*
Agree	*53%*	*52%*
Disagree	*31%*	*35%*
Neither	*6%*	*9%*
Don't know	*10%*	*4%*

(13) Do you or members of your family work at Vickers?

Yes	No
55%	44%

More than half the population of Barrow either work at Vickers or have a member of their family who works at Vickers. This very heavy economic dependence on Vickers was an important factor in designing the subsequent peace action campaign.

ii. Cross tabulations

(1) Do you think Trident is necessary for the defence of this country?

		Yes	No	Don't know	
		50%	36%	12%	
(3) Do you think	*Less Secure*	1%	10%	0%	13%
that building Trident	*Stable*	12%	10%	4%	27%
at Barrow makes	*More Secure*	35%	10%	5%	51%
the future of Vickers	*Don't know*	1%	4%	1%	8%
(5) Would you prefer	*Yes*	24%	35%	7%	69%
Vickers to build something	*No*	17%	0%	1%	18%
rather than Trident?	*Don't know*	8%	1%	3%	13%
(7) Do you	*Yes*	33%	1%	1%	35%
think this expenditure	*No*	9%	33%	5%	49%
on Trident is justified?	*Don't know*	7%	2%	4%	14%

More than 90% of those who thought Trident "necessary for the defence of this country" also thought it made the future of Vickers stable or more secure, 70% feeling Vickers would be more secure. Those who did not think Trident necessary for the defence of the country divide very differently with equal numbers feeling Vickers would be less sure, stable and more secure.

It is no surprise that 98% of those who did not think Trident necessary for the defence of the country would prefer Vickers to build something else, as compared to 48% of those who did think Trident necessary. Only one third of those who did think Trident necessary would not prefer Vickers to build something else.

While two thirds of those who thought Trident necessary for national defence thought the expenditure on Trident justified, 18% did not. This ambivalence provided an important input to the peace action campaign.

(1) Do you think Trident is necessary for the defence of this country?

		Yes	No	Don't know	
		50%	36%	12%	
(10) What do the	*Right*	30%	26%	6%	64%
initials C.N.D.stand for	*Wrong*	20%	9%	5%	36%
(11) Do you think that	*Yes*	16%	19%	5%	42%
Barrow and District CND					
has made you more aware	*No*	30%	14%	4%	49%
of nuclear weapons and					
the Trident programme	*DK*	3%	2%	2%	8%
(12) Do you	*Yes*	5%	22%	2%	29%
support	*No*	39%	10%	6%	55%
C.N.D.?	*Don't know*	6%	3%	2%	14%
(13) Do you or a member of	*Yes*	29%	20%	5%	55%
your family work at Vickers	*No*	21%	16%	5%	44%

Sixty percent of those who thought Trident necessary knew what the initials CND stood for as compared to 75% of those who were opposed to Trident.

More than half of those opposed to Trident thought Barrow CND had made them more aware of nuclear weapons as compared to one third of those who supported Trident.

Just over a quarter of those who opposed Trident do not support CND while one sixth of those who said they supported CND also supported Trident! While it is possible to oppose Trident and not support CND, the explanations for supporting CND and Trident are more difficult. Factors such as uncertainty as to the goals of CND and confusion as to whether Trident is a British or US weapon are likely to be relevant.

For those who worked or had a family member work at Vickers 53% supported Trident and 37% did not. This compares to 48% support and 36% opposition among those not connected through work to Vickers.

(1) Do you think Trident is necessary for the defence of this country?

		Yes	No	Don't know	
		50%	36%	12%	
Sex	*Male*	27%	21%	3%	52%
	Female	22%	15%	8%	48%
Age range	*Under 20*	5%	5%	2%	13%
	20-30	9%	10%	4%	25%
	30-40	12%	8%	2%	23%
	40-50	8%	4%	1%	14%
	50-60	7%	3%	0%	10%
	over 60	7%	3%	1%	12%

More than half the men questioned supported Trident, while less than half the women took that view. However about 40% of the men opposed Trident as compared to about one third of the women. As with most items the percentage of "Don't knows" is higher among women.

The under 20s are equally divided in their attitude towards Trident with the same number of people answering yes as no. The 20-30 age group is the only one where more people answered no (40%) than yes (36%). As the age groups get older the percentages of each group against Trident lessens while the percentage for steadily increases. Thus the 30-40 age group has about 50% yes, 33% no; the 40-50 age group has 66% yes, 33% no; the 50-60 age group has 70% yes, 30% no; as does the over 60 age group.

(3) Do you think that building Trident at Barrow makes the future of Vickers

		Less secure 13%	Stable 27%	More secure 51%	Don't know 8%	
(5) Would you	Yes	11%	19%	29%	6%	69%
prefer Vickers to	No	0%	3%	13%	0%	18%
build something	DK	0%	3%	8%	1%	13%
rather than Trident.						

All who thought building Trident would make Vickers future less secure prefered Vickers to build something else as did 70% of those who answered stable. About three quarters of those who didn't want Vickers to build something else thought Trident made the future for Vickers more secure. Thus there appeared to be a connection between preferring Vickers to build Trident or something else, and seeing the future of Vickers as more or less stable.

(3) Do you think that building Trident at Barrow makes the future of Vickers

		Less secure 13%	Stable 27%	More secure 51%	Don't know 8%	
(7) Do you think	Yes	1%	7%	25%	0%	35%
this expenditure	No	11%	14%	17%	5%	49%
on Trident is	DK	0%	4%	8%	1%	14%
justified?						
(12) Do you	Yes	9%	8%	8%	2%	29%
support CND?	No	2%	14%	35%	3%	55%
	DK	1%	4%	6%	1%	14%

About three quarters of those who thought Trident expenditure justified felt that building Trident at Barrow would make the future of Vickers more secure compared to just over one third of those who thought the expenditure was not justified. Well over 90% of those who thought Vickers would be less secure did not think the expenditure justified.

About 70% of those who thought Trident made the future of Vickers less secure supported CND and 70% of those who thought Trident made the future of Vickers more secure did not support CND. CND supporters were roughly equally represented in each of the three options (less secure, stable, more secure) while opponents of CND were heavily skewed towards the view that building Trident made the future of Vickers more secure with more than 60% of them answering more secure and less than 4% less secure.

(3) Do you think that building Trident at Barrow makes the future of Vickers

		Less secure 13%	Stable 27%	More secure 51%	Don't know 8%	
(13) Do you or a member of your family work at Vickers	Yes	6%	15%	28%	4%	55%
	No	6%	11%	22%	4%	44%
Sex	Male	7%	14%	27%	4%	52%
	Female	5%	12%	24%	3%	48%
Age	*Under 20*	0%	4%	7%	1%	13%
	20-30	4%	7%	12%	1%	25%
	30-40	3%	6%	10%	2%	23%
	40-50	1%	3%	7%	1%	14%
	50-60	1%	2%	6%	0%	10%
	Over 60	1%	2%	7%	1%	12%

Interestingly there appears to be no significant difference between those who work at Vickers or who have a family member who works at Vickers, and those who do not. The same is true for the crosstabulation with sex.

The findings with regard to age structure are quite similar to those obtained from crosstabulations with item (1) (attitude towards Trident and national defence). None of the under 20s thought "less secure"; the 20-30 and 30-40 age groups are the only groups where less than half answer "more secure" and more than 10% of each of these groups thought "less secure"; while the older age groups are all skewed towards the view "more secure".

(5) Would you prefer Vickers to build something rather than Trident?

		Yes	No	Don't know	
		69%	18%	13%	
(7) Do you think this	Yes	14%	15%	5%	35%
expenditure on Trident	No	45%	1%	2%	49%
is justified?	DK	8%	1%	5%	14%
(10)What do the initials	Right	45%	11%	6%	64%
CND stand for	Wrong	22%	6%	5%	36%
(11) Do you think that	Yes	32%	4%	4%	42%
Barrow CND has	No	30%	12%	6%	49%
made you more aware of ...	DK	4%	0%	2%	8%

Those who thought the expenditure on Trident justified were roughly equally divided on prefering Vickers to build something other than Trident, while those who did not think the expenditure justified overwhelmingly prefered Vickers to build something else. More than half of those who didn't know if they would prefer Vickers to build something else thought the expenditure was not justified. The overwhelming majority of those who didn't prefer Vickers to build something else thought the expenditure justified.

While knowledge of what the initials CND stand for is not related to item (5) four out of five of those who thought Barrow CND had made them more aware prefered Vickers to build something else as compared to three out of five of those who didn't think Barrow CND had made them more aware. About two thirds of those who did not prefer Vickers to build something else did not think Barrow CND had made them more aware. A separate cross tabulation confirmed that virtually all of those who supported CND prefered

Vickers to build something else, while more than 60% of non CND supporters took the same view.

Cross tabulations of item (5) against item (13), work at or family work at Vickers, and of item (5) against age revealed no significant differences. There were some variations with regard to sex, 71% of men, as compared to 63% of women, prefering Vickers to build something else.

(5) Would you prefer Vickers to build something rather than Trident?

		Yes	No	Don't know	
		69%	18%	13%	
Sex	*Male*	37%	9%	5%	52%
	Female	30%	9%	7%	48%

(7) Do you think this expenditure on Trident is justified?

		Yes	No	Don't know	
		35%	49%	14%	
(11)Do you think that	Yes	10%	25%	5%	42%
Barrow CND has made you	No	22%	20%	6%	49%
more aware of.....	DK	1%	3%	3%	8%
(12)Do you support CND?	Yes	2%	24%	2%	29%
	No	29%	18%	7%	55%
	DK	3%	5%	4%	14%

About 60% of those who thought Barrow CND had made them more aware of nuclear issues didn't think the expenditure justified as compared to about 40% of those who didn't think Barrow CND had made them more aware. About two thirds of those who thought the expenditure justified did not think Barrow CND had made them more aware while about one half of those who thought

120

the expenditure not justified thought Barrow CND had made them more aware of nuclear issues.

While there was no linkage for item (7) with working at Vickers there were differences with regard to age and sex.

(7) Do you think this expenditure on Trident is justified?

		Yes	*No*	*Don't know*	
		35%	*49%*	*14%*	
Sex	*Male*	*18%*	*27%*	*6%*	*52%*
	Female	*16%*	*21%*	*8%*	*48%*
Age	*under 20*	*3%*	*6%*	*3%*	*13%*
	20-30	*6%*	*14%*	*4%*	*25%*
	30-40	*8%*	*11%*	*3%*	*23%*
	40-50	*5%*	*6%*	*1%*	*14%*
	50-60	*5%*	*4%*	*0%*	*10%*
	over 60	*6%*	*5%*	*1%*	*12%*

51% of men, as compared to 44% of women, did not think the expenditure on Trident justified. With regard to age there is a characteristic relationship between age group and attitude towards expenditure on Trident. Roughly half those under 20 didn't think the expenditure justified as compared to 60% in the 20-30 age range. This percentage steadily drops as we go through the age ranges to about 40% for the 50-60 and over 60 groups. At the same time the percentage who do think it justified rises by age group from 25% for the under 20 group to 50% for the over 50 groups.

(10) What do the initials C.N.D. stand for?

		Right 64%	Wrong 36%	
(13)Do you or members of your	*Yes*	*37%*	*17%*	*55%*
family work at Vickers?	*No*	*26%*	*17%*	*44%*
Sex	*Male*	*41%*	*11%*	*52%*
	Female	*22%*	*23%*	*48%*
Age	*under 20*	*8%*	*4%*	*13%*
	20-30	*16%*	*7%*	*25%*
	30-40	*15%*	*7%*	*23%*
	40-50	*9%*	*4%*	*14%*
	50-60	*6%*	*3%*	*10%*
	over 60	*6%*	*6%*	*12%*

Knowledge of what the letters CND stand for, like other knowledge items discussed later, show some characteristic features. Those who work at Vickers or have a family member work at Vickers are more likely to know what CND represents. Similarly about half the women didn't know what the initials meant while 80% of the men did. In terms of age groups 60% of under 20, 64% of 20-30, 65% of 30-40, 64% of 40-50, 60% of 50-60 and 50% of over 60 knew the correct answer. This trend, though slight, follows a similar pattern to several other items.

(11) Do you think that Barrow and District CND has made you more aware of nuclear weapons?

	Yes	*No*	*Don't know*	
	42%	*49%*	*8%*	
(13) Do you or members of *Yes*	*22%*	*29%*	*3%*	*55%*
your family work at Vickers? *No*	*19%*	*19%*	*4%*	*44%*

122

Sex					
	Male	19%	30%	3%	52%
	Female	22%	19%	4%	48%

Age					
	under 20	6%	5%	1%	13%
	20-30	12%	10%	1%	25%
	30-40	9%	12%	1%	23%
	40-50	4%	8%	1%	14%
	50-60	4%	6%	0%	10%
	over 60	4%	6%	1%	12%

For item 11 a clear majority of those who worked, or have a family member work, at Vickers do not think Barrow CND has made them more aware of nuclear matters, while among those not connected to Vickers equal numbers answered yes and no. Again there are clear sex differences with about 60% of men answering no to this question whilst for women more answered yes than no. There are also age differences, for the under 20 and 20-30 age groups more people answered yes than no, while for all other age groups more answered no.

(12) Do you support C.N.D.?

	Yes	No	Don't know
	29%	55%	14%

		Yes	No	Don't know	
(13) Do you or members of	Yes	16%	32%	7%	55%
your family work at Vickers	No	13%	23%	6%	44%

Sex					
	Male	16%	30%	5%	52%
	Female	13%	25%	8%	48%

Age					
	under 20	3%	5%	3%	13%
	20-30	9%	12%	3%	25%
	30-40	6%	13%	3%	23%
	40-50	3%	9%	1%	14%
	50-60	3%	6%	0%	10%
	over 60	3%	7%	1%	12%

These crosstabulations provided some valuable information. While 29% support C.N.D. there was no significant difference in levels of support among those who work or have a family member working at Vickers (16 out of 55) , and those who do not work for or have a family member working for Vickers (13 out of 44). In a town where 55% of our sample worked at or had a family member working at Vickers this is an important finding.

About one third of the men, as compared to 28% of the women, supported CND, while 57% of the men, as compared to 53% of the women didn't support CND. The greatest support for CND, 36%, came from the 20-30 age group.

iii Knowledge and Attitudes

Questions 2,4,6 and 8 tested a persons knowledge about Trident. A knowledge index was constructed by scoring one for each correct answer. A person with no correct answers scored zero, while correctly answering all questions gave a score of 4. The overall breakdown of the knowledge index and the various cross tabulations are as follows.

		Knowledge Score					
		0	1	2	3	4	
		28%	30%	25%	9%	5%	
Sex	Male	8%	14%	15%	9%	4%	52%
	Female	19%	15%	9%	0%	1%	48%
(1) Do you think Trident	Yes	15%	15%	12%	5%	1%	50%
is necessary for the	No	7%	11%	9%	3%	3%	36%
defence of this country?	DK	6%	2%	2%	0%	0%	12%
(2) Do you think	Less Secure	2%	3%	4%	1%	1%	13%
that building	Stable	5%	7%	7%	3%	2%	27%
Trident at	More Secure	18%	16%	11%	4%	1%	51%
Barrow makes the	Don't know	2%	2%	1%	0%	0%	8%
future of Vickers							

The wide spread lack of knowledge about the Trident programme among the people of Barrow in 1985 is apparent from these figures. Just 5% of the sample gave correct answers to all four knowledge questions while nearly sixty percent scored zero or one. There is in addition a very definite sex difference with some 70% of women scoring zero or 1, and 2% of women scoring 3 or 4, as compared to 25% of men scoring 3 or 4.

The knowledge index differentiates between those who thought Trident necessary for the defence of the country and those who did not. 60% of those answering yes had knowledge scores of zero or one compared to 50% of those answering no. 12% of those answering yes had scores of three or four compared to 17% of those answering no.

For question 2, more than two thirds of those answering more secure had knowledge score of zero or one as compared to 5/13 ths (just over one third) of those answering less secure and 4/9ths of those answering stable. Similarly about one in six of those answering less secure or stable have knowledge scores of three or four as compared to one in ten of those answering more stable.

The knowledge score does not differentiate between responses to questions (5) or (7). But in terms of age groups the under twenties were the least informed with 80% having knowledge scores of zero or one, while the 40-50 age group were the best informed with more than 20% having scores of 3 or 4.

In the case of question 9, what government spending priorities should be, those with a knowledge score of 3 or 4 placed health and education as their top priorities, while the 5% who placed military expenditure first had knowledge scores of zero or one and were all over 40. As one might also expect all those with knowledge scores of 3 or 4 knew what the initials C.N.D. stand for (although this question was not a part of the knowledge score) and 50% of those who did not know had a knowledge score of zero.

3 The campaign

The 1985 survey formed the basis for extended discussions with Barrow CND. A number of aspects of the survey were important in designing the subsequent campaign in Barrow. To begin with it was clear that the level of basic knowledge about the number of submarines to be built, the cost of the Trident program, and the percentage of the Trident budget that would be spent in the United States was low. There were important gender differences with regard to knowledge, women having much less knowledge than men. In addition the general level of knowledge about the Trident program was related to support for Trident.

Since the CND group were anxious to change the opinions of people who at that time were in favour of Trident some specific analyses of selected groups were undertaken. For example the survey had revealed that there was 9% of the sample who thought Trident was necessary for the defence of the country but who did not think the expenditure on Trident was justified. It was felt that individuals in this group were possibly more likely to change their minds on Trident than, for example, those in favour of Trident who felt the expenditure was justified. Consequently this target group was compared to the whole sample in a number of ways including age structure, the security of Vickers (3), alternative production at Vickers (5), and estimated cost of Trident (6). The following tables summarize the findings from this comparison, the figures in brackets being for the whole sample.

(A) Age structure.

Under 20	20-30	30-40	40-50	50-60	Over 60
10%(13%)	*25%(25%)*	*23%(23%)*	*18%(14%)*	*12%(10%)*	*9%(12%)*

There was a slight, but not strong, indication that the 40-60 group 30% (24%) is over represented in the group.

(B) Security of Vickers

(3) Do you think that building Trident at Barrow makes the future of Vickers

Less Secure	Stable	More Secure	Don't know
5%(13%)	*25%(27%)*	*63%(51%)*	*5%(8%)*

Some 63% of the target group felt Trident made the future more secure as compared to 51% of the whole sample while 5% felt it made Vickers future less secure as compared to 13% of the whole sample.

(C) Alternative production at Vickers

(5) Would you prefer Vickers to build something rather than Trident?

Yes	*No*	*Don't know*
78%(69%)	*12%(18%)*	*9%(13%)*

The target group is more supportive of alternative production than the whole sample.

(D) Estimated cost of Trident (knowledge item)

(6) The estimated cost of Trident is (in millions of pounds £M)

£1M	*£10M*	*£100M*	*£1,000M*	*£10,000M*	*Don't know*
0%(0%)	*12%(8%)*	*20%(10%)*	*14%(13%)*	*14%(25%)*	*30%(42%)*

Despite the fact that the target group did not think the expenditure on Trident justified, they underestimated this expenditure much more than the whole sample. For the whole sample and for other sub samples knowledge of this item is related to support for Trident being necessary, those getting the right answer tending to be more opposed to Trident.

This type of analysis of possible target groups suggested that a campaign stressing the cost of Trident and the local possibilities for alternative production that would make the future of Vickers more secure should be undertaken. In focusing on cost the campaign would also concentrate on the fact that half the Trident budget was to be spent in the United States.

Campaigning materials focusing on these issues were prepared by the group who used posters, leaflets, newspaper advertisements and public meetings as the main campaigning techniques. The campaigning material included the following items.

(1) A bright pink day glow (fluorescent) poster with the words "£12,000,000,000 The Choice is YOURS!"

(2) A leaflet with simple graphics stressing the cost of the Trident program was £12,000,000,000 (12 Billion pounds) and that with the Trident program half of this (6 billion pounds) would go straight to the United States and the other half would be spent in the UK on submarines and warheads.

(3) Four local Barrow newspaper advertisements, three of them stressing central information from the leaflet. One of the three advertisements used graphics from the leaflet, one stressed the number of hospitals, schools and houses that could be built with the money, and the third the number of jobs that could be created per million pounds building Trident, building conventional defence equipment, building homes, or if spent on the health service or in education. The 4th advertisement stressed the destructive power of Trident.

The campaign included leafleting, public meetings and advertising using the carefully focused set of materials.

4 The 1986 follow up survey

Just over one year later on Saturday May 31st a second survey was carried out at the same time and locations in which 401 people were interviewed by about the same number of interviewers. The break down of the samples are as follows:

	Under 20	20-30	30-40	40-50	50-60	Over 60
1985 Male	6%	13%	11%	8%	6%	6%
1985 Female	6%	11%	12%	5%	4%	5%
1985 Total	13%	25%	23%	14%	10%	12%
1986 Male	4%	10%	14%	7%	5%	10%
1986 Female	5%	9%	11%	6%	6%	8%
1986 Total	10%	19%	25%	14%	11%	18%

In 1985 the sample comprised 52% men and 48% women, in 1986 53% men and 47% women. The 1986 sample contained a lower percentage in the 20-30 age group and a higher percentage in the over 60 age group. During the period between the two surveys the order for the first Trident submarine was confirmed, any subsequent orders being defered most probably until after the then upcoming general election; Vickers Shipyard was privatised and came under the control of a local consortia; and Barrow CND had conducted their public information campaign designed to increase opposition in Barrow to the Trident system.

General results for items included in both surveys

The 1985 survey asked 13 questions, the 1986 survey 14. Some of the questions were asked in both surveys and this section gives a summary of the findings for those items. Other questions were only asked in one of the surveys, and where relevant these are included. Cross tabulations are included in a separate section of this report.

(A) Do you think Trident is necessary for the defence of this country?

	Yes	No	Don't know
1985	50%	36%	12%
1986	42%	43%	13%

During the year between the two surveys the 14% majority support for Trident in the 1985 survey has vanished. The 1986 survey shows the people of Barrow divided on the question "Do you think Trident is necessary for the defence of this country" with 42% answering yes and 43% no. If we again compare the results from this question with the Marplan national poll the shift in attitude in Barrow compared to the national average is striking.

Marplan = M: Britain is safer having its own nuclear weapons.
Barrow Trident Question (A) = T

	1985M	1985T	1986M	1986T
Agree	52%	50%	50%	42%
Disagree	35%	36%	36%	43%
Neither/Don't know	13%	12%	13%	13%

It must of course be remembered that the two questions are different, but nevertheless it is of some interest that the dramatic shift in attitude in Barrow with regard to Trident is not present in the general national attitude with regard to nuclear weapons.

(B) Do you think that building Trident at Barrow makes the future of Vickers

	Less Secure	Stable	More Secure	Don't know
1985	13%	27%	51%	8%
1986	10%	29%	49%	10%

A very similar pattern is evident for both surveys on this question.

(C) How many Trident submarines are to be built at Barrow? (1985)
If the total Trident programme is completed, how many Trident submarines are to be built at Barrow? (1986)

The 1986 question had to be modified to take into account the 1986 contract to build one submarine, with the remaining 3 boats to be commissioned probably after the then upcoming election.

	1	4	8	16	Don't know
1985	2%	27%	9%	2%	57%
1986	3%	32%	8%	1%	52%

In 1985 about one quarter of the sample knew that 4 Trident submarines were to be built, while in 1986 nearly one third gave the correct answer. The number of Don't knows had also dropped between 1985 to 1986.

(D) Would you prefer Vickers to build something rather than Trident?

	Yes	No	Don't know
1985	69%	18%	13%
1986	68%	18%	13%

There is clearly a constant preference for building something other than Trident at Vickers, 7 out of 10 expressing this opinion in both 1985 and 1986.

(E) The estimated cost of Trident is (in millions of pounds £M)

£1M	£10M	£100M	£1,000M	£10,000M	DK (1985)
0%	8%	10%	13%	25%	42%
0%	6%	12%	18%	7%	53%
£12M	£120M	£1.2B	£12B	£120B	DK (1986)

In the 1986 survey the actual number was written under the million or billion number, thus £12,000,000,000 was written under the correct answer £12 Billion. Unfortunately comparisons on this question are very difficult. The cost estimate for Trident had escalated from £10,000 Million in 1985 to £12,000 Million in 1986; the 1985 survey made the mistake of putting £10,000 Million as the highest possible choice; the 1986 survey included £120 Billion as its top option. Thus, for example, while 25% guessed the highest figure in 1985, 7% guessed this figure in 1986 with 18% guessing the second highest (correct figure).

(F) Do you think this expenditure on Trident is justified?

	Yes	*No*	*Don't know*
1985	*35%*	*49%*	*14%*
1986	*34%*	*54%*	*10%*

In 1985 Trident was accepted as a "necessary but undesirable evil", since 50% thought Trident necessary for the defence of the country, 69% would rather build something else, and only 35% thought the expenditure justified. By May 1986 42% thought Trident necessary for the defence of the country as compared to 43% who disagreed, 69% would rather build something else, and a majority, 54% Don't think the expenditure is justified.

(G) What percentage of this cost will be spent in the United States?

	None	*About 20%*	*About 50%*	*About 70%*	*Don't know*
1985	*1%*	*10%*	*22%*	*16%*	*49%*
1986	*0%*	*8%*	*28%*	*14%*	*47%*

During the year the percentage knowing the correct answer to this question rose from 22% to 28%. On the six questions that are directly comparable between the two samples, no change was apparent on two and significant change occurs for four. The people of Barrow were constant with regard to building Trident and the security of Vickers, with nearly 80% thinking Vickers was either stable or more secure as a result of Trident; and constant with regard to prefering Vickers to build something rather than Trident, with nearly 70% holding that view.There has been an increase of knowledge about

Trident with more people knowing how many submarines are to be built and more knowing that about half the cost will be spent in the United States. At the same time there has been a marked swing against Trident being necessary for the defence of this country from a 50% Yes, 36% No position of support to a 42% Yes, 43% No split; and a swing against the expenditure on Trident being justified from a 35% Yes, 49% No position to a 34% Yes, 54% No situation.

The 1986 survey included some items that were not in the 1985 survey.

3. Do you think the future of Vickers is secure if Trident is cancelled?

Yes	No	Don't know
33%	42%	23%

The response to this question clearly illustrates the concern that exists in Barrow for the future of the Vickers yards if Trident were cancelled.

9. Where would 1 Billion pounds create the most jobs?
(1=most jobs, 2, 3, 4, 5 = least jobs)

	Defence	Health	Trident	Education	Housing
1	13%	32%	3%	13%	35%
2	6%	25%	5%	26%	13%
3	7%	15%	5%	23%	22%
4	39%	6%	11%	8%	5%
5	8%	2%	46%	7%	5%
DK	24%	16%	27%	19%	16%

Some of the interviewers reported difficulty in administering this question, feeling that some respondents answered this in terms of what they would prefer rather than in terms of how many jobs would be created per Billion pounds, so care must be taken in interpretation. The preference for Housing and Health, and then for Education is in any case clear (as was the case in the 1985 survey where the question asked for priorities). Trident ranks number 5 in nearly half the cases.

10. Do you work at Vickers?		11.Does a member of your family work at Vickers?	
Yes	*No*	*Yes*	*No*
22%	77%	44%	55%

In the 1985 survey one question asked

13. Do you or a member of your family work at Vickers?

Yes	*No*
55%	44%

When 1986 (10) is cross tabulated against 1986 (11) the survey shows that 13% work at Vickers and also have a member of their family working at Vickers. Thus had the survey asked 1985 (13) the result would have been 44%+13%=57%, a very comparable figure.

In 1986 the survey also asked

(12) Are you a shareholder in Vickers?

Yes	*No*
31%	68%

Roughly one adult in three claims to be a shareholder. The final series of items on the questionnaire concerned material used by Barrow CND in their Public Information Campaign and comparable newspaper articles and adverts. The question asked

(13) Recently there has been a lot of publicity surrounding Trident and Vickers. Please tell the interviewer which of the newspaper and poster items you have seen?

	Item A	*Item B*	*Item C*	*Item D*	*Item E*	*Item F*
Yes	50%	11%	26%	9%	28%	12%
No	48%	87%	72%	80%	71%	86%

	Item G	*Item H*	*Item I*	*Item J*	*Item K*
Yes	29%	22%	19%	13%	29%
No	70%	77%	80%	86%	69%

Item A, CND's pink day glow poster "£12,000,000,000. The Choice is YOURS!" is clearly the item most remembered, 50% having seen it previously. Item K, the leaflet distributed by Barrow CND was the second most remembered item together with Item G, "Vickers land Trident order" (an article in the local press). About 30% remembered seeing these. The most remembered CND advert, H with 22%, included graphics from the CND leaflet, and the second most popular CND advert, I with 19%, also included some items from the leaflet. The remaining two CND adverts, B with 11% and F with 12% are comparable to Item J, a National Express Bus advert, which scored 13%. While Item F echoed parts of the leaflet it was the smallest CND advert, while the larger advert B did not relate to the leaflet in any way (it described the destructive power of Trident).

Cross tabulations

(A) Do you think Trident is necessary for the defence of this country?

		1985 Yes	1986 Yes	1985 No	1986 No	1985 Don't know	1986 Don't know	1985	1986
		50%	42%	36%	43%	12%	13%		
(B)Do you	Less Secure	1%	0%	10%	8%	0%	0%	13%	10%
think that	Stable	12%	11%	10%	13%	4%	4%	27%	29%
building Tri-	More Secure	35%	28%	10%	13%	5%	7%	51%	49%
dent at Barrow	Don't know	1%	1%	4%	7%	1%	0%	8%	10%
makes the future									
of Vickers:									
(C)Would you	Yes	24%	21%	35%	37%	7%	8%	69%	68%
prefer Vickers to									
Build something	No	17%	14%	0%	2%	1%	1%	18%	18%
rather than									
Trident	Don't know	8%	5%	1%	3%	3%	3%	13%	12%

(F) Do you think this expenditure on Trident is justified?	Yes	33%	30%	1%	1%	1%	2%	35%	34%
	No	9%	7%	33%	38%	5%	7%	49%	54%
	Don't Know	7%	4%	2%	2%	4%	3%	14%	10%

Between 1985 and 1986 there is a drop from 35% to 28% in those who think building Trident at Barrow makes the future of Vickers more secure and who think Trident is necessary for defence. There is great consistency between the two surveys, in both years only one third of those who thought Trident necessary would not prefer Vickers to build something else.

In 1985 33% thought that Trident was necessary for defence and that the expenditure on Trident was justified, in 1986 this decreased to 30%. In 1985 33% opposed Trident and thought the expenditure not justified, in 1986 this increased to 38%. A key element of the CND campaign had been expenditure on Trident and this shift in opinion on these two items meant a central goal of the public information campaign mounted by the peace group had been achieved during the year, a year in which the 50% to 36% majority had been changed to a 43% to 42% position against Trident.

(A) Do you think Trident is necessary for the defence of this country?

		1985	1986	1985	1986	1985	1986		
		Yes		No		Don't Know			
		50%	42%	36%	43%	12%	13%		
								1985	1986
Sex									
	Male	27%	23%	21%	23%	3%	5%	52%	53%
	Female	22%	18%	15%	19%	8%	7%	48%	47%
Age range	Under 20	5%	3%	5%	4%	2%	1%	13%	10%
	20-30	9%	5%	10%	9%	4%	3%	25%	18%
	30-40	12%	9%	8%	11%	2%	3%	23%	25%
	40-50	8%	5%	4%	6%	1%	1%	14%	14%

50-60	7%	5%	3%	4%	0%	1%	10%	11%
over 60	7%	11%	3%	6%	1%	0%	12%	18%
(D) How many Trident submarines are to be built at Barrow? 1	1%	1%	1%	1%	0%	0%	2%	3%
4	14%	14%	10%	14%	2%	3%	27%	32%
8	4%	3%	3%	3%	0%	1%	4%	8%
16	1%	1%	1%	0%	0%	0%	2%	1%
DK	28%	20%	20%	23%	8%	8%	57%	52%
(G) What percentage of this cost will be spent in the United States? None	0%	0%	0%	0%	0%	0%	1%	0%
About 20pct	6%	4%	3%	3%	0%	0%	10%	8%
About 50pct	11%	12%	9%	12%	1%	2%	22%	28%
About 70pct	6%	3%	9%	8%	0%	1%	16%	14%
Don't know	25%	20%	14%	18%	9%	8%	49%	7%

For both men and women in the two samples support for Trident has eroded. When age is considered, the 1986 sample has a lower percentage of the 20 to 30 age group, 18% as compared to 25%, and a higher percentage of the over 60 age group, 18% as compared to 12%. In both samples support for Trident is higher in the over 60 sample than in the under 20 sample and it is therefore likely that the actual swing against Trident is higher than that recorded, whichever sample is more accurate.

For the knowledge item (D), number of submarines to be built, the distribution for those who think Trident is necessary for the defence of this country is very similar between 1985 and 1986, with the exception of a drop of 8% for the Don't knows on knowledge about how many submarines are to be built. For those who do not think Trident is necessary for the defence of this country, the percentage who do know that 4 submarines are to be built has risen from 10% to 14%, and the Don't know number of submarines from 20% to 23%. Knowledge on this item has increased, with 32% now knowing the correct answer as compared to 27% in 1985.

For knowledge item (G), percentage of money to be spent in the United States, the pattern is similar to item (D) with an increase in knowledge concerning percentage spent in the United States, this increase being distributed in the anti Trident column between the correct answer, 50%, and Don't know.

Some items were asked in 1986 and not 1985. These cross tabulate with (A) as follows.

(A) Do you think Trident is necessary for the defence of this country?

		Yes	No	Don't know	
		42%	43%	13%	
(3) Do you think the	*Yes*	8%	22%	2%	33%
future of Vickers is	*No*	23%	13%	6%	42%
secure if Trident is	*DK*	9%	8%	4%	23%
cancelled?					
10. Do you work	*Yes*	11%	8%	2%	22%
at Vickers?	*No*	30%	35%	11%	77%
(11) Does a member	*Yes*	21%	18%	4%	44%
of your family	*No*	20%	24%	9%	55%
work at Vickers?					
(12) Are you a	*Yes*	16%	11%	2%	31%
shareholder in	*No*	25%	31%	10%	68%
Vickers?					

Those who think Trident is necessary for defence tend to think the future of Vickers is not secure if Trident is cancelled, while those who do not think Trident necessary for defence tend to think the future of Vickers is secure if Trident is cancelled. Those who work at Vickers, or have a member of their family work at Vickers, or are a shareholder in Vickers are more likely to think Trident necessary for defence.

The cross tabulations for the advertisements, leaflets and newspaper articles follow. Yes means they were seen, no means not.

(A) Do you think Trident is necessary for the defence of this country?

		Yes	No	Don't know	
		42%	43%	13%	
A "£12,000,000,000	Yes	19%	24%	6%	50%
THE CHOICE IS YOURS"	No	22%	18%	7%	48%
(Day Glow Poster)					
B CND Trident advertisement	Yes	5%	5%	0%	11%
with 7,200 Hiroshimas	No	36%	38%	12%	87%
C Trident Clinched	Yes	12%	11%	2%	26%
Newspaper Article	No	29%	32%	10%	72%
D Trident "threat"	Yes	7%	9%	1%	19%
as boffins quit	No	34%	33%	12%	80%
Newspaper Article					
E TRIDENT DEAL IS	Yes	13%	10%	3%	28%
UNIQUE	No	28%	32%	10%	71%
Newspaper Article					
F £12,000,000,000 IS THE	Yes	5%	5%	1%	12%
ESTIMATED COST OF TRIDENT	No	36%	37%	12%	86%
(CND advertisement)					
G Vickers land Trident	Yes	13%	12%	3%	29%
order(Newspaper article)	No	28%	30%	10%	70%
H CND Uncle Sam taking	Yes	10%	10%	1%	22%
half the money	No	31%	32%	12%	77%
(CND Advertisement)					
I CND Hospitals,Schools	Yes	7%	10%	1%	19%
Houses Advertisement	No	34%	33%	12%	80%

J National Express	*Yes*	*7%*	*4%*	*1%*	*13%*
Newspaper advert	*No*	*34%*	*39%*	*12%*	*86%*
K CND door to door	*Yes*	*10%*	*16%*	*2%*	*29%*
leaflet	*No*	*31%*	*27%*	*11%*	*69%*

Items A and K appear to be related to views concerning Trident. In both cases those who remember seeing them are more likely not to think Trident necessary for the defence of this country. These two items are also the two items people remembered seeing the most, item A being remembered by 50%, item K by 29%.

5 Conclusion

The action research project described in this paper is unique in the British peace movement and while it is possible to argue that the public information campaign conducted by Barrow CND produced spectacular results in terms of attitudinal changes, it is also possible that other factors played a major part in the shifts of opinion that occurred.

On the one hand there is the evidence from the national Marplan survey of attitudes that suggests very little shift in attitudes about British nuclear weapons, the Marplan survey was published three months after the 1986 Barrow survey. The fact that the percentage figures for Marplan 1985 are so close to the 1985 Barrow survey for attitudes towards Trident adds strength to this argument.

Evidence from the Barrow surveys further strengthens the claim that Barrow CND had a major impact on public attitudes. One of the knowledge questions concerned the percentage of the cost of Trident that would be spent in the United States. The fact that 50% of £12 Billion UK expenditure on Trident was to be spent in the USA was not actively publicised by either Vickers or the British Government. The Barrow CND campaign was centered on this fact, using devices such as pictures of "Uncle Sam" taking half the twelve "Billion Pound Coins". In the 1985 pre campaign survey 22% of the population knew that 50% of the UK Trident expenditure would be spent in the USA, in the 1986 survey 28%.

Counter to this argument is the fact that the Chernobyl nuclear reactor accident took place between the two surveys, an accident that deposited significant amounts of radiation on the Lakedistrict Mountains close to Barrow. In addition while Marplan did not publish survey materials on Trident, they did publish data on US Ground Launched Cruise Missiles then based at Greenham Common. In answer to the question

The Government should tell the American Government to remove its cruise missiles from British soil the 1985 and 1986 responses were

	1985	*1986*
Agree	*50*	*54*
Disagree	*32*	*36*
Neither	*9*	*10*
Don't know	*5*	*4*

While the shift in opinion for this item is about one half of the shift recorded in Barrow, it could be argued that the Barrow campaign in its "Americanisation" of the Trident issue, magnified an "anti US nuclear weapon trend" that already existed. The other results from Marplan discussed above do not show such a large shift for "UK Nuclear weapons".

Peace movements can be viewed in a variety of ways, as causes and as effects. Many who participate in such activities may do so to protest or be counted. Many believe, at least during the action, that peace action can influence others, can change minds and even hearts. It would be wrong to argue that peace action must be functional in the sense that it should "work", that is it should achieve goals, change minds, influence policy. Much peace action can be, and almost certainly is, undertaken for other reasons. The approach adopted in this article is not meant to imply just a "functional" view of peace action, although it is meant to suggest ideas for those who wish to explore functional possibilities.

The apparent schism between "expressive" and "functional" peace action is of considerable importance as the history of "non violence" illustrates. There are many examples of functional non violent activists adopting violence when non violence "fails". For spiritual pacifists such failure is impossible because non violence is a way of life. For functional pacifists and "nuclear pacifists", an action research methodology may be a valuable tool in creating a peaceful world, not only with regard to military relations between states but also for peace between people.

Bibliography

Literature Survey on Peace Movement Studies

Compiled by Katsuya Kodama

A number of scholars have mentioned and regretted scarcity of literature on peace movement studies. It may be safely said that the peace movements have been relatively ignored as study subjects by peace researchers, sociologists, political scientists, etc. Recently however, this trend has been challenged. Since the surprising growth of new peace movements in early 1980s, special attention has been directed toward peace movements not only by the general public but also by intellectuals.

The result is a growing number of books, articles, journals and papers on peace movements. The study group on peace movement research of the International Peace Research Association (IPRA) has listed such contributions in an effort to make an extensive, annotated bibliography in this area. The following bibliography is an interim report from this effort and it contains only references in English.

It is by no means copmplete. For instance, the reader may also turn to the peace movement bibliography in *World Encyclopedia of Peace* edited by Ervin Laszlo and Jong Youl Yoo (Volume 4), Pergamon Press 1986. Therefore, we would be very grateful if you could inform us about your own publications and those of others concerning various aspects of peace movements which are missing here. Please send such references to Katsuya Kodama at LUPRI so we can produce the most comprehensive and up-to-date final version.

	AUTHOR(S)	YEAR	TITLE OF BOOK	PUBLISHER	PLACE
1	BAHRO, Rudolf	1986	BUILDING THE GREEN MOVEMENT	GMP PUBLISHERS Ltd	LONDON
2	BAHRO, Rudolf	1984	FROM RED TO GREEN; INTERVIEW WITH NEW LEFT REVIEW	VERSO EDITION	LONDON
3	BAHRO, Rudolf	1983	SOCIALISM AND SURVIVAL	HERETIC	LONDON
4	BAHRO, Rudolf	1981	THE ALTERNATIVE IN EASTERN EUROPE	VERSO EDITION	LONDON
5	BAMBA, Nobuya & HOWES, John F.	1978	PACIFISM IN JAPAN	MINERVA PRESS	KYOTO
6	BARNABY, Frank & THOMAS, G.P. (eds.)	1982	THE NUCLEAR ARMS RACE	FRANCES PINTER	LONDON
7	BARNES, Samuel, KASSE, Max, et al.(eds.)	1979	POLITICAL ACTION; MASS PARTICIPATION IN FIVE WESTERN DEMOCRACIES	SAGE	LONDON
8	BELL, Daniel	1976	THE COMING OF POST-INDUSTRIAL SOCIETY	PENGUIN	HARMONDSWORTH
9	BELL, Daniel	1960	THE END OF IDEOLOGY	FREE PRESS	GLENCOE
10	BENEWICK, Robert & SMITH, Trevor (eds.)	1972	DIRECT ACTION AND DEMOCRATIC POLITICS	ALLEN & UNWIN	LONDON
11	BERRIGAN, Daniel (ed.)	1985	FOR SWORDS INTO PLOWSHARE	PISCATAWAY	
12	BOGGS, Carl	1986	SOCIAL MOVEMENTS AND POLITICAL POWER	TEMPLE UNIVERSITY PRESS	PHILADELPHIA, U.S.A.
13	BROCK, Peter	1968	A HISTORY OF PACIFISM	PRINCETON UNIVERSITY PRESS	PRINCETON, N.J.
14	BROCK, Peter	1972	PACIFISM IN EUROPE TO 1914	PRINCETON UNIVERSITY PRESS	PRINCETON, N.J.
15	BROCK, Peter	1968	PACIFISM IN THE UNITED STATES; FROM THE COLONIAL ERA TO THE FIRST WORLD WAR	PRINCETON UNIVERSITY PRESS	PRINCETON, N.J.
16	BROCK, Peter	1970	TWENTIETH CENTURY PACIFISM	VAN NOSTRAND	
17	BRUCE-BRIGGS, B. (ed.)	1979	THE NEW CLASS?	TRANSACTION BOOKS	NEW BRUNSWICK, N.J.
18	BUSSEY, Gertrude & TIME Margaret	1965	WOMEN'S INTERNATIONAL LEAGUE FOR PEACE AND FREEDOM, 1915-1965	GEORGE ALLEN & UNWIN	

	AUTHOR(S)	YEAR	TITLE OF BOOK	PUBLISHER	PLACE
19	CAPRA, Frijof & SPRETNAK, Charlene	1984	GREEN POLITICS	E.P. DUTTON	NEW YORK
20	CEADEL, Martin	1980	PACIFISM IN BRITAIN, 1918-45	OXFORD	LONDON
21	CHATFIELD, C. & van den DUNGEN, P. (eds.)	1988	PEACE MOVEMENTS AND POLITICAL CULTURES	THE UNIV. OF TENESSEE PRESS/ KNOXVILLE	U.S.A.
22	CHATFIELD, Charles	1971	FOR PEACE AND JUSTICE; PACIFISM IN AMERICA, 1914-1941	UNIVERSITY OF TENNESSEE PRESS	KNOXVILLE
23	CHATFIELD, Charles (ed.)	1973	PEACE MOVEMENTS IN AMERICA	SCHOCKEN	NEW YORK
24	CLOTFELTER, James & PRYSBY, Charles L.	1980	POLITICAL CHOICES	HOLKT, RINEHART, WINSTON	NEW YORK
25	COHEN, Mitchell & HALE, Dennis	1966	THE NEW STUDENT LEFT; AN ANTHOLOGY	BEACON PRESS	BOSTON
26	COLE, P. M.& TAYLOR, W. J.,Jr. (eds.)	1983	THE NUCLEAR FREEZE DEBATE; ARMS CONTROL ISSUES FOR THE 1980S	WESTVIEW PRESS	BOULDER, COLO.
27	COONEY, R. & MICHALOWSKI, H.	1979	THE POWER OF THE PEOPLE	PEACE PRESS	U.S.A.
28	CREIGHTON, Colin & SHAW, Martin (eds.)	1987	THE SOCIOLOGY OF WAR AND PEACE	MACMILLAN	LONDON
29	CURTI, Merle	1959	PEACE OR WAR; THE AMERICAN STRUGGLE 1636-1936	CANNER	
30	DAHRENDORF, Ralf	1959	CLASS AND CLASS CONFLICT IN INDUSTRIAL SOCIETY	STANFORD UNIVERSITY PRESS	STANFORD, CA.
31	DAUBERT, V. L. & MORAN, S. E.	1985	ORIGINS, GOALS, AND TACTICS OF THE U.S. ANTI-NUCLEAR PROTEST MOVEMENT	RAND REPORT N-2192-SL	SANT MONICA
32	DeBENDETTI, Charles	1980	THE PEACE REFORM IN AMERICAN HISTORY	INDIANA UNIVERSITY PRESS	BLOOMINGTON
33	DRIVER, Christopher	1964	THE DISARMERS; A STUDY IN PROTEST	HODDER AND STOUGHTON	
34	END PAMPHLET	1983	THE PEACE MOVEMENT IN TURKEY	END	LONDON
35	EVAN, Willinam M. & HILGARTNER, Stephan	1987	THE ARMS RACE AND NUCLEAR WAR	PRENTICE HALL	ENGLEWOOD CLIFFS N.J.
36	EVANS, Sara	1979	PERSONAL POLITICS; THE ROOTS OF WOMEN'S LIBERATION IN THE CIVIL RIGHTS MOVEMENT AND THE NEW LEFT	ALFRED A. KNOPF	NEW YORK

	AUTHOR(S)	YEAR	TITLE OF BOOK	PUBLISHER	PLACE
3 7	FINN, James (ed.)	1968	PROTEST; PACIFISM AND POLITICS	RANDOM HOUSE	NEW YORK
3 8	FRANKEL, Boris	1987	THE POST-INDUSTRIAL UTOPIANS	POLITY PRESS	CAMBRIDGE, UK
3 9	FREMAN, Jo (ed.)	1983	SOCIAL MOVEMENTS OF THE SIXTIES AND SEVENTIES	LONGMAN	NEW YORK
4 0	GALTUNG, Johan	1984	THERE ARE ALTERNATIVES	SPOKESMAN	NOTTINGHAM, ENGLAND
4 1	GAMSON, William	1975	THE STRATEGY OF SOCIAL PROTEST	DORSEY	HOMEWOOD, IL.
4 2	GOULDNER, Alvin W.	1985	AGAINST FRAGMENTATION	OXFORD UNIVERSITY PRESS	NEW YORK & OXFORD
4 3	GOULDNER, Alvin W.	1979	THE FUTURE OF INTELLECTUALS AND THE RISE OF THE NEW CLASS	SEABURY	NEW YORK
4 4	GREER, Herb	1964	MUD PIE; THE CND STORY	MAX PARRISH	
4 5	GRUNBERG, Danielle	1982	THE MOSCOW INDEPENDENT PEACE GROUP	MERLIN PRESS & END	LONDON
4 6	HABERMAS, Jürgen	1973	LEGITIMATION CRISIS	BEACON PRESS	BOSTON
4 7	HARFORD, Barbara & HOPKINS, Sarah (eds.)	1984	GREENHAM COMMON; WOMEN AT THE WIRE	THE WOMEN'S PRESS	
4 8	HAYDEN, Tom	1969	REBELLION AND REPRESSION	WORLD PUBLISHING COMPANY	NEW YORK & CLEVELAND
4 9	HEBERLE, Rudolf	1951	SOCIAL MOVEMENT; AN INTRODUCTION TO POLITICAL SOCIOLOGY	APPLETON-CENTURY-CROFTS	NEW YORK
5 0	HERZOG, Arthur	1965	THE WAR/PEACE ESTABLISHMENT	HARPER AND ROW	
5 1	HIRST, Margaret	1923	THE QUAKERS IN PEACE AND WAR	SWARTHMORE PRESS	LONDON
5 2	HOROWITZ, Louis	1970	THE STRUGGLE IS THE MESSAGE; THE ORGANIZATION AND IDEOLOGY OF THE ANTI-WAR MOVEMENT	BERKELEY	
5 3	INGLEHART, Ronald	1977	THE SILENT REVOLUTION; CHANGING VALUES AND POLITICAL STYLES AMONG WESTERN PUBLICS	PRINCETON UNIVERSITY PRESS	PRINCETON, N.J.
5 4	JACOBS, Paul & LANDAU, Saul	1966	THE NEW RADICALS	VINTAGE BOOKS	NEW YORK

	AUTHOR(S)	YEAR	TITLE OF BOOK	PUBLISHER	PLACE
5 5	KALTEFLEITER, W. & PFALTZGRAFF, R. L.	1985	THE PEACE MOVEMENTS IN EUROPE & THE UNITED STATES	CROOM HELM	LONDON & SYDNEY
5 6	KELLY, Petra	1984	FIGHTING FOR HOPE	SOUTH END PRESS	BOSTON
5 7	KODAMA, Katsuya & VESA, Unto (eds.)	1989 (in print)	TOWARDS A COMPARATIVE ANALYSIS OF PEACE MOVEMENTS	DARTMOUTH	HAMPSHIRE
5 8	KRIESBERG, L.	1981	SOCIAL MOVEMENTS AND SOCIAL CHANGE. CONFLICT AND CHANGE	JAI PRESS	GREENWICH AND LONDON
5 9	KÖSZEGI, Ferenc & THOMPSON, E.P.	1982	THE NEW HUNGARIAN PEACE MOVEMENT	MERLIN PRESS	LONDON
6 0	LAQUEUR, Walter & HUNTER, Robert (eds.)	1985	EUROPEAN PEACE MOVEMENTS AND THE FUTURE WESTERN ALLIANCE	TRANSACTION BOOKS	NEW BRUNSWICK, N.J.
6 1	LARKEY, George	1972	STRATEGY FOR A LIVING REVOLUTION	FREEMAN	
6 2	LASCH, Christopher	1969	THE AGONY OF THE AMERICAN LEFT	ALFRED A. KNOPF	NEW YORK
6 3	LONG, S.L.(ed.)	1981	THE HANDBOOK OF POLITICAL BEHAVIOR	PLENUM	NEW YORK
6 4	LOVENDUSKI, Joni	1986	WOMEN AND EUROPEAN POLITICS; CONTEMPORARY FEMINISM AND PUBLIC POLICY	HARVESTER	BRIGHTON
6 5	LYND, Staughton (ed.)	1966	NON-VIOLENCE IN AMERICA; A DOCUMENTARY HISTORY	THE BOBBS-MERRILL Co.	INDIANAPOLIS AND NEW YORK
6 6	MANN, Michael	1973	CONSCIOUSNESS AND ACTION AMONG THE WESTERN WORKING CLASS	MACMILLAN	LONDON
6 7	MARCHAND, C. Roland	1972	THE AMERICAN PEACE MOVEMENT AND SOCIAL REFORM 1898-1918	PRINCETON UNIVERSITY PRESS	PRINCETON, N.J.
6 8	MARTIN, David	1965	PACIFISM; A HISTORICAL AND SOCIOLOGICAL STUDY	ROUTLEDGE, KEGAN AND PAUL	LONDON
6 9	MATTAUSCH, John	1989	A COMMITMENT TO CAMPAIGN; A SOCIOLOGICAL STUDY OF CND	MANCHESTER UNIVERSITY PRESS	MANCHESTER & NEW YORK
7 0	McALLISTER, Pam	1982	REWEAVING THE WEB OF LIFE: FEMINISM AND NONVIOLENCE	NEW SOCIETY PUBLISHER	PHILADELPHIA, U.S.A.
7 1	MELUCCI, Alberto	1989	NOMADS OF THE PRESENT	HUTCHINSON RADIUS	LONDON
7 2	MENDLOVITZ, Saul H. & WALKER, R.B.J.	1987	TOWARDS A JUST WORLD PEACE: PERSPECTIVES FROM SOCIAL MOVEMENTS	BUTTERWORTHS	LONDON

	AUTHOR(S)	YEAR	TITLE OF BOOK	PUBLISHER	PLACE
7 3	MILLS, C.W.	1959	THE POWER ELITE	OXFORD UNIVERSITY PRESS	NEW YORK
7 4	MINNION, J. & BOLSOVR, P. (eds.)	1983	THE CND STORY	ALLISON & BUSBY	LONDON
7 5	MOOREHEAD, Caroline	1987	TROUBLESOME PEOPLE; ENEMIES OF WAR 1916-1986	HAMISH HAMILTON	LONDON
7 6	MOTTOLA, Kari (ed.)	1983	NUCLEAR WEAPONS AND NORTHERN EUROPE; PROBLEMS AND PROSPECTS OF ARMS CONTROL	FINNISH INST. INTER-NATIONAL AFFAIRS	HELSINKI
7 7	NUTTALL, Geoffrey	1971	CHRISTIAN PACIFISM IN HISTORY	SEABURY	NEW YORK
7 8	OBERSCHALL, Anthony	1873	SOCIAL CONFLICT AND SOCIAL MOVEMENTS	PRENTICE HALL	ENGLEWOOD CLIFFS N.J.
7 9	OFFE, Claus	1984	CONTRADICTIONS OF THE WELFARE STATE	HUTCHINSON	LONDON
8 0	OVERY, Bob	1982 1983	HOW EFFECTIVE ARE PEACE MOVEMENTS?	HOUSEMANS & BEACON (revised)	LONDON, NEW YORK
8 1	PARKIN, Frank	1979	MARXISM AND CLASS THEORY; A BOURGEOIS CRITIQUE	TAVISTOCK	LONDON
8 2	PARKIN, Frank	1968	MIDDLE CLASS RADICALISM; THE SOCIAL BASES OF THE BRITISH CAMPAIGN FOR NUCLEAR DISARMAMENT	MANCHESTER UNIVERSITY PRESS	MANCHESTER
8 3	PETERSON, H. C. & FITE, Gilbert	1957	OPPONETS OF WAR 1917-1918	UNIVERSITY OF WISCONSIN	
8 4	POLAK, Fred	1972	IMAGE OF THE FUTURE, two volumes	JOSSEY-BASS/ELSEVIER	SAN FRANCISCO
8 5	PORRITT, Jonathon	1985	SEEING GREEN; THE POLITICS OF ECOLOGY EXPLAINED	BASIL BLACKWELL	LONDON
8 6	ROSE, Richard (ed.)	1980	ELECTORAL PARTICIPATION	SAGE	LONDON
8 7	SCHUMPETER, Joseph	(1942) 1962	CAPITALISM, SOCIALISM AND DEMOCRACY	HARPER	NEW YORK
8 8	SELZNICK, Philip	1960	THE ORGANIZATIONAL WEAPON	FREE PRESS	NEW YORK
8 9	SHARP, Gene	1985	MAKING EUROPE UNCONQUERABLE; THE POTENTIAL OF CIVILIAN-BASED DETERRENCE AND DEFENCE	BALLINGER	CAMBRIDGE, MASS.
9 0	SHARP, Gene	1973	POLITICS OF NON-VIOLENT ACTION (3 voumes)	PORTER SARGENT	BOSTON

	AUTHOR(S)	YEAR	TITLE OF BOOK	PUBLISHER	PLACE
9 1	SHAW, M. (ed.)	1984	WAR, STATE AND SOCIETY	MACMILLAN	LONDON
9 2	SMELSER, Neil	1963	THEORY OF COLLECTIVE BEHAVIOR	FREE PRESS	NEW YORK
9 3	TAYLOR, R. & YOUNG, N. (eds.)	1987	CAMPAIGNS FOR PEACE: THE BRITISH PEACE MOVEMENTS IN THE 20TH CENTURY	MANCHESTER UNIVERSITY PRESS	MANCHESTER
9 4	TAYLOR, Richard & PRITCHARD, Colin	1980	THE PROTEST MAKERS	PERGAMON	NEW YORK & LONDON
9 5	TEODORI, Massimo (ed.)	1969	THE NEW LEFT; A DOCUMENTARY HISTORY	THE BOBBS-MERRILL Co.	INDIANAPOLIS AND NEW YORK
9 6	THOMPSON, E. P. & SMITH, D.	1982	PROTEST AND SURVIVE	PENGUIN	LONDON
9 7	TOURAINE, Alain	1971	THE POST-INDUSTRIAL SOCIETY	RANDOM HOUSE	NEW YORK
9 8	TOURAINE, Alain	1981	THE VOICE AND THE EYE; AN ANALYSIS OF SOCIAL MOVEMENTS	CAMBRIDGE UNIVERSITY PRESS	
9 9	WALLER, Douglas C.	1987	CONGRESS AND THE NUCLEAR FREEZE	THE UNIVERSITY OF MASSACHUSETTS PRESS	MASSACHUSETTS, U.S.A.
1 0 0	WILTSHIRE, Anne	1985	MOST DANGEROUS WOMEN; FEMINIST PEACE CAMPAIGNERS OF THE GREAT WAR	PANDORA PRESS	
1 0 1	WITTNER, Lawrence	1969	REBELS AGAINST WAR; THE AMERICAN PEACE MOVEMENT 1941-1960	COLUMBIA UNIVERSITY PRESS	
1 0 2	YOUNG, Nigel	1977 1978	AN INFANTILE DISORDER	ROUTLDGE & KEGAN WESTVIEW PRESS	PAUL BOULDER
1 0 3	YOUNG, Nigel	1981	PROBLEMS AND POSSIBILITIES OF PEACE	HOUSEMANS	LONDON
1 0 4	YOUNG, Nigel	1976	WAR RESISTANCE AND THE NATION STATE	ANN ARBOR	MICHIGAN
1 0 5	ZALD, Mayer N. & MCCARTHY, John D. (eds)	1987	SOCIAL MOVEMENTS IN AN ORGANIZATIONAL SOCIETY	TRANSACTION BOOKS	NEW BRUNSWICK, N.J.
1 0 6	ZALD, Mayer. N. & MCCARTHY, John. D.	1979	THE DYNAMICS OF SOCIAL MOVEMENTS; RESOURCE MOBILIZATION, SOCIAL CONTROL, AND TACTICS	WINTHROP	CAMBRIDGE, MASS.

	AUTHOR(S)	YEAR	TITLE OF ARTICLE	INCLUDED IN
1	AGØY, Nils Ivar	(in print)	THE NORWEGIAN PEACE MOVEMENT AND THE QUESTION OF CONSCIENTIOUS OBJECTION TO MILITARY SERVICE 1885-1922	"TOWARDS A COMPARATIVE ANALYSIS OF PEACE MOVEMENTS", KODAMA, K. & VESA, U. (eds.) DARTMOUTH
2	ALFSEN, Erik	1982	A NUCLEAR WEAPON FREE ZONE IN THE NORDIC COUNTRIES	BULLETIN OF PEACE PROPOSALS, VOL.13, NO.3.
3	ALGER, Chadwick F	1987	A GRASSROOTS APPROACH TO LIFE IN PEACE; SELF-DETERMINATION IN OVERCOMING PEACELESSNESS	BULLETIN OF PEACE PROPOSALS, VOL.18, NO.3
4	ALGER, Chadwick F	1985	CREATING LOCAL INSTITUTIONS IN THE UNITED STATES FOR SUSTAINED PARTICIPATION IN PEACE BUILDING	PEACE AND THE SCIENCES, NO.1/2
5	ALGER, Chadwick F	1988	PERCEIVING, ANALYZING AND COPING WITH THE LOCAL-GLOBAL NEXUS	INTERNATIONAL SOCIAL SCIENCE JOURNAL
6	ALGER, Chadwick F.& MENDLOVITZ, Saul H.	1987	GRASSROOTS INITIATIVES; THE CHALLENGE OF LINKAGES	"TOWARDS A JUST WORLD PEACE", MENDLOVITZ, Saul H. and WALKER, R.B.J.(eds.) BUTTERWORTHS, LONDON
7	ALLEN, Vic	1985	THE POTSDAM CONFERENCE AND THE WESTERN PEACE MOVEMENT	PEACE AND THE SCIENCES, NO.3
8	ANTOLA, Esko	1983	COMMUNISTS, NEUTRALISTS, UNILATERALISTS, RITUALISTS; AN ANATOMY OF WAR AGAINST PEACE MOVEMENTS IN WESTERN EUROPE IN 1980'S	A PAPER PRESENTED AT THE 10TH GENERAL CONFERENCE OF IPRA, GYÖR, HUNGARY
9	APUNEN, Osmo	1980	NORDIC NUCLEAR FREE ZONE	COOPERATION AND CONFLICT, VOL.15. NO.4
10	APUNEN, Osmo	1980	THREE 'WAVES' OF THE KEKKONEN PLAN & NORDIC SECURITY IN THE 1980's	BULLETIN OF PEACE PROPOSALS, VOL.11, NO.1
11	ARATO, Andrew & COHEN, Jean	1982	THE PEACE MOVEMENT AND WESTERN EUROPEAN SOVEREIGNTY	TELOS, 51, SPRING
12	ASMUS, Ronald D.	1983	IS THERE A PEACE MOVEMENT IN THE GDR?	ORBIS, VOL. 27, NO.4

	AUTHOR(S)	YEAR	TITLE OF ARTICLE	INCLUDED IN
1 3	BAHrO. Rudolf	1982	THE SPD AND THE PEACE MOVEMENT	NEW LEFT REVIEW, NO.131
1 4	BARTH, Magne	1982	THE MOVEMENT FOR A NUCLEAR WEAPON FREE ZONE IN THE NORDIC REGION	BULLETIN OF PEACE PROPOSALS, VOL.13, NO.2.
1 5	BEER, Francis A.	1986	A LONG BROAD VIEW OF THE ANTI-NUCLEAR WEAPONS MOVEMENT; ENVIRONMENT, ACTORS, AND RESEARCH	A PAPER PRESENTED AT THE 11TH GENERAL CONFERENCE OF IPRA, UNIVERSITY OF SUSSEX, U.K.
1 6	BELL, Daniel	1979	THE NEW CLASS; A MUDDLED CONCEPT	"THE NEW CLASS?", BRUCE-BRIGGS, B. (ed.) TRANSACTION, NEW BRUNSWICK, NJ.
1 7	BENGTSSON, Eva Stina	1968	SOME POLITICAL PERSPECTIVES OF ACADEMIC RESERVE OFFICERS	JOURNAL OF PEACE RESEARCH, VOL.5, NO.3
1 8	BENHABIB, Seyla	1982	THE WEST GERMAN PEACE MOVEMENT AND ITS CRITICS	TELOS, 51, SPRING
1 9	BERMAN, Russel	1982	OPPOSITION TO REARMAMENT AND WEST GERMAN CULTURE	TELOS, 51, SPRING
2 0	BERMAN, Russel	1982	THE PEACE MOVEMENT AND ITS CRITICS' CRITICS; REPLY TO BREINES AND BENHABIB	TELOS, 52, SUMMER
2 1	BERMAN, Russel	1983	THE PEACE MOVEMENT DEBATE; PROVISIONAL CONCLUSIONS	TELOS, 57, FALL
2 2	BETTY, Reardon	1983	A GENDER ANALYSIS OF MILITARISM	INTERNATIONAL PEACE RESEARCH NEWSLETTER, VOL. XXI, NO.2
2 3	BINTER, Josef	1985	PROBLEMS AND PERSPECTIVES OF THE PEACE MOVEMENT IN WESTERN EUROPE AND IN AUSTRIA	PEACE AND THE SCIENCES, NO.1/2
2 4	BLEE, Kathleen M.	1985	MOBILITY AND POLITICAL ORIENTATION ; AN ANALYSIS OF SEX DIFFERENCES	SOCIOLOGICAL PERSPECTIVES, 28 (3)

	AUTHOR(S)	YEAR	TITLE OF ARTICLE	INCLUDED IN
25	BOGGS, Carl	1986	THE GREEN ALTERNATIVE AND THE STRUGGLE FOR A POST-MARXIST DISCOURSE	THEORY AND SOCIETY, 15
26	BOSERUP, Anders & IVERSEN, Claus	1966	DEMONSTRATIONS AS A SOURCE OF CHANGE - A STUDY OF BRITISH AND DANISH EASTER MARCH	JOURNAL OF PEACE RESEARCH, VOL.3, NO.4
27	BOUDON, Raymond	1971	SOURCES OF STUDENT PROTEST IN FRANCE	ANNUALS OF THE AAPSS 395
28	BOULDING, Elise	1983	PEACE MOVEMENT IN U.S.A.	INTERNATIONAL PEACE RESEARCH NEWSLETTER, VOL.XXI, NO.3
29	BREDOW, Wilfried von	1982	THE PEACE MOVEMENT IN THE FEDERAL REPUBLIC OF GERMANY	ARMED FORCES AND SOCIETY, VOL.9, NO.1, FALL
30	BREINES, Paul	1982	ON BERMAN AND SOCIAL MOVEMENTS	TELOS, 51, SPRING
31	BRINT, Steven	1984	'NEW CLASS' AND CUMULATIVE TREND EXPLANATIONS OF THE LIBERAL POLITICAL ATTITUDES OF PROFESSIONALS	AMERICAN JOURNAL OF SOCIOLOGY, 90
32	BRINT, Steven	1985	THE POLITICAL ATTITUDES OF PROFESSIONALS	ANNUAL REVIEW OF SOCIOLOGY, VOL.11
33	BRODIN, Katarina	1981	THE NORDIC COUNTRIES AND THE PROSPECTS FOR A NUCLEAR WEAPON FREE ZONE	CONTEMPORARY HISTORY, NO.1386, JULY
34	BUKOVSKY, Vladimir	1982	THE PEACE MOVEMENT AND THE SOVIET UNION	COMMENTARY, 73(5) MAY
35	BURRIS, Val	1986	THE DISCOVERY OF THE NEW MIDDLE CLASS	THEORY AND SOCIETY, 15
36	BUKLIN, Wilhelm P.	1985	THE GERMAN GREENS; THE POST-INDUSTRIAL NON-ESTABLISHED AND THE PARTY SYSTEM	INTERNATIONAL POLITICAL SCIENCE REVIEW, 6 (4), OCTOBER

	AUTHOR(S)	YEAR	TITLE OF ARTICLE	INCLUDED IN
3 7	BYRD, Peter	1985	THE DEVELOPMENT OF THE PEACE MOVEMENT IN BRITAIN	"EUROPEAN PEACE MOVEMENTS & THE FUTURE OF THE WESTERN ALLIANCE", LAQUEUR, W. & HUNTER, R. (eds.) TRANSACTION BOOK, N.J.
3 8	BAR, Monsignor Drs R.P.	1982	CHRISTIANITY AND DETERRENCE	NATO REVIEW, NO.1
3 9	BÖGE, Volker & WILKE, Peter	1986	PEACE MOVEMENT AND UNILATERAL DISARMAMENT - OLD CONCEPTS IN A NEW VIEW	A PAPER PRESENTED AT THE 11TH GENERAL CONFERENCE OF IPRA, UNIVERSITY OF SUSSEX, U.K.
4 0	CAPITANCHIK, David	1983	PUBLIC OPINION AND NUCLEAR WEAPONS IN EUROPE	ARMS CONTROL 4 (2)
4 1	CEADEL, Martin	1987	THE PEACE MOVEMENT BETWEEN THE WARS; PROBLEMS OF DEFINITION	"CAMPAIGN FOR PEACE:BRITISH PEACE MOVE-MENTS IN THE TWENTIETH CENTURY" TAYLOR, R.& YOUNG,N.(eds.)MANCHESTER UNIV. PRESS
4 2	CHAPER, Tony	1985	POLITICS AND THE PERCEPTION OF RISK; A STUDY OF THE ANTI-NUCLEAR MOVEMENTS IN BRITAIN AND FRANCE	WEST EUROPEAN POLITICS, VOL.8, NO.1
4 3	CHATFIELD, Charles	1978	PACIFISM	"THE ENCYCLOPEDIA OF AMERICAN FOREIGN POLICY STUDIES OF THE PRINCIPAL MOVEMENTS & IDEAS", VOL.2
4 4	CHICKERING, Roger	1988	WAR, PEACE, AND SOCIAL MOBILIZATION IN IMPERIAL GERMANY; PATRIOTIC SOCIETIES, THE PEACE MOVEMENT, AND SOCIALIST LABOR	"PEACE MOVEMENTS & POLITICAL CULTURES", CHATFIELD, C.& DUNGEN, P. (eds.) THE UNIVERSITY TENNESSEE PRESS/ KNOXVILLE
4 5	CLECAK, Peter	1981	THE MOVEMENT AND ITS LEGACY	SOCIAL RESEARCH, VOL.48, NO.3
4 6	CLOTFELTER, James	1986	DISARMAMENT MOVEMENTS IN THE UNITED STATES	JOURNAL OF PEACE RESEARCH, VOL.23, NO.2
4 7	COATES, Ken	1987	LISTENING FOR PEACE	END PAPERS SPECIAL 2
4 8	COATES, Ken	1982	NUCLEAR FREE ZONES IN BRITAIN	END PAPERS, SPRING

	AUTHOR(S)	YEAR	TITLE OF ARTICLE	INCLUDED IN
4 9	COATES, Ken	1984	NUCLEAR-FREE ZONES: PROBLEMS AND PROSPECTS	END PAPERS 8, SUMMER
5 0	COATES, Ken	1986	PEACE MOVEMENTS UNITED: ALLIANCES DIVIDED	END PAPERS 11, WINTER
5 1	COHEN, Jean	1983	RETHINKING SOCIAL MOVEMENTS	BERKELEY JOURNAL OF SOCIOLOGY, VOL.XXVII
5 2	COHEN, Jean	1985	STRATEGY OR IDENTITY: NEW THEORETICAL PARADIGMS AND CONTEMPORARY SOCIAL MOVEMENTS	SOCIAL RESEARCH, VOL.52, NO.4
5 3	COHEN, Jean & ARATO, Andrew	1984	THE GERMAN GREEN PARTY; A MOVEMENT BETWEEN FUNDAMENTALISM AND MODERNISM	DISSENT, (SUMMER)
5 4	COTGROVE, Stephen & DUFF, Andrew	1980	ENVIRONMENTALISM, MIDDLE CLASS RADICALISM AND POLITICS	SOCIOLOGICAL REVIEW, 28
5 5	CRAMER, J., EYEMAN, R. & JAMISON, A.	1987	THE KNOWLEDGE INTERESTS OF THE ENVIRONMENTAL MOVEMENT AND ITS POTENTIAL FOR INFLUENCING THE DEVELOPMENT OF SCIENCE	THE SOCIAL DIRECTION OF PUBLIC SCIENCES. SOCIOLOGY OF SCIENCES YEARBOOK XI
5 6	CRIPPEN, Timothy; LOPRETO, Joseph	1981	DIMENSIONS OF SOCIAL MOBILITY AND POLITICAL BEHAVIOR	JOURNAL OF POLITICAL AND MILITARY SOCIOLOGY, 9 (2) FALL
5 7	DAVIS, Jacquelyn K.	1985	THE US NUCLEAR FREEZE CAMPAIGN: FACTS AND FALLACIES	"EUROPEAN PEACE MOVEMENTS & THE FUTURE OF THE WESTERN ALLIANCE", LAQUEUR, W. & HUNTER, R.(eds.) TRANSACTION BOOKS, N.J.
5 8	DAY, Graham & ROBBINS, David	1987	ACTIVISTS FOR PEACE; THE SOCIAL BASIS OF A LOCAL PEACE MOVEMENT	"THE SOCIOLOGY OF WAR AND PEACE", CREIGHTON, C. & SHAW, M. (eds.) MACMILLAN PRESS, LONDON
5 9	DEBENEDETTI, Charles	1988	AMERICAN PEACE ACTIVISM, 1945-1985	"PEACE MOVEMENTS & POLITICAL CULTURES", CHATFIELD, C.& DUNGEN, P. (eds.) THE UNIVERSITY TENNESSEE PRESS/ KNOXVILLE
6 0	DeBENEDETTI, Charles	1983	ON THE SIGNIFICANCE OF CITIZEN PEACE ACTIVISM; AMERICA 1961-1975	PEACE AND CHANGE, 9, SUMMER

	AUTHOR(S)	YEAR	TITLE OF ARTICLE	INCLUDED IN
61	DeBENEDETTI, Charles	1978	THE AMERICAN PEACE MOVEMENT AND THE NATIONAL SECURITY STATE 1941-1971	WORLD AFFAIRS, 141(2) FALL
62	DRAGO, Antonio	1986	ITALIAN PEACE MOVEMENT; AN ANALYSIS FROM A NONVIOLENT POINT OF VIEW	A PAPER PRESENTED AT THE 11TH GENERAL CONFERENCE OF IPRA, UNIVERSITY OF SUSSEX, U.K.
63	DRAGO, Antonio	1983	TOWARDS A PROGRAM FOR NON-VIOLENT POPULAR DEFENSE	GANDHI MARG, VOL.5
64	DUBET, F., TOURAINE, A. & WIEVIORKA, M.	1982	A SOCIAL MOVEMENT; SOLIDARITY	TELOS, 53, FALL
65	DUMONT, Joel-Francois	1985	THE PEACE MOVEMENT IN FRANCE	"EUROPEAN PEACE MOVEMENTS & THE FUTURE OF THE WESTERN ALLIANCE", LAQUEUR, W. & HUNTER, R. (eds.) TRANSACTION BOOK, NJ.
66	DUNGEN, Peter van den	1987	CRITICS AND CRITICISMS OF THE BRITISH PEACE MOVEMENT	"CAMPAIGN FOR PEACE;BRITISH PEACE MOVEMENTS IN THE TWENTIETH CENTURY" TAYLOR, R.& YOUNG,N.(eds.)MANCHESTER UNIV. PRESS
67	DWYER, Lynn E.	1983	STRUCTURE AND STRATEGY IN THE ANTI-NUCLEAR MOVEMENT	"SOCIAL MOVEMENTS OF THE SIXTIES AND SEVENTIES", FREEMAN, Jo (ed.) LONGMAN, NEW YORK
68	DÜLFFER, Jost	1988	CITIZENS AND DIPLOMATS; THE DEBATE ON THE FIRST HAGUE CONFERENCE (1899) IN GERMANY	"PEACE MOVEMENTS & POLITICAL CULTURES", CHATFIELD, C.& DUNGEN, P. (eds.) THE UNIVERSITY TENNESSEE PRESS/ KNOXVILLE
69	EDER, Klaus	1985	THE "NEW SOCIAL MOVEMENTS"; MORAL CRUSADES, POLITICAL PRESSURE GROUPS, OR SOCIAL MOVEMENTS?	SOCIAL RESEARCH, VOL.52, NO.4
70	EGLIN, Josephine	1987	WOMEN AND PEACE; FROM THE SUFFRAGISTS TO THE GREENHAM WOMEN	"CAMPAIGN FOR PEACE;BRITISH PEACE MOVEMENTS IN THE TWENTIETH CENTURY" TAYLOR, R.& YOUNG,N.(eds.)MANCHESTER UNIV. PRESS
71	EICHNER, Klaus	(in print)	THE U.S. AND THE WEST GERMAN PEACE MOVEMENTS OF THE EIGHTIES; AN EMPIRICAL COMPARISON	"TOWARDS A COMPARATIVE ANALYSIS OF PEACE MOVEMENTS", KODAMA, K. & VESA, U. (eds.) DARTMOUTH
72	ENGLISH, Robert	1984	EASTERN EUROPE'S DOVES	FOREIGN POLICY, NO.56

	AUTHOR(S)	YEAR	TITLE OF ARTICLE	INCLUDED IN
7 3	EVANS, G. Russell	1983	PACIFISM AND THE US CHURCHES	JOURNAL OF SOCIAL, POLITICAL AND ECONOMIC STUDIES, 8 (3) FALL
7 4	EVERTS, Philip P.	1988	THE IMPACT OF THE PEACE MOVEMENT ON PUBLIC OPINION AND POLICY-MAKING; THE CASE OF THE NETHERLANDS	"A JUST PEACE THROUGH TRANSFORMATION" ALGER, Chadwick & STOHL, Michael (eds.) WESTVIEW PRESS, BOULDER & LONDON
7 5	FARBER, Mient Jan	1982	THE PEACE MOVEMENT IN EUROPE	GANDHI MARG, VOL.4: 2-3
7 6	FEHER, Ferenc & HELLER, Agnes	1983	ON BEING ANTI-NUCLEAR IN SOVIET SOCIETIES	TELOS, 57, FALL
7 7	FESHBACH, Seymour	(in print)	CHANGING WAR-RELATED ATTITUDES	"PSYCHOLOGY AND THE PREVENTION OF NUCLEAR WAR", WHITE, Ralph(ed.)
7 8	FESHBACH, Seymour & WHITE, Michael J.	1986	INDIVIDUAL DIFFERENCES IN ATTITUDES TOWARDS NUCLEAR ARMS POLITICS: SOME PSYCHOLOGICAL AND SOCIAL POLITY CONSIDERATION	JOURNAL OF PEACE RESEARCH, VOL.23, NO.2
7 9	FINGER, Matthias	(in print)	THE NEW PEACE MOVEMENT AND ITS CONCEPTION OF POLITICAL COMMITMENT	"TOWARDS A COMPARATIVE ANALYSIS OF PEACE MOVEMENTS", KODAMA, K. & VESA, U. (eds.) DARTMOUTH
8 0	FINN, James	1985	THE PEACE MOVEMENT IN THE UNITED STATES	"EUROPEAN PEACE MOVEMENTS & THE FUTURE OF THE WESTERN ALLIANCE", LAQUEUR, W. & HUNTER, R.(eds.) TRANSACTION BOOK, N.J.
8 1	FISKE, S., PRATTO, F. & PAVELCHAK, M.	1983	CITIZENS' IMAGES OF NUCLEAR WAR; CONTENT AND CONSEQUENCES	JOURNAL OF SOCIAL ISSUES, VOL.39, NO.1
8 2	FLYNN, Gregory	1983	PUBLIC OPINION AND ATLANTIC DEFENCE	NATO REVIEW, NO.5
8 3	FONTANEL, Jacques	1986	AN UNDEVELOPED PEACE MOVEMENT: THE CASE OF FRANCE	JOURNAL OF PEACE RESEARCH, VOL.23, NO.2
8 4	FOREST, Jim & HERBY, Peter	1982	HOLLANDITIES; EUROPE'S PLAGUE OF PEACE	IFFOR REPORT, JAN.

	AUTHOR(S)	YEAR	TITLE OF ARTICLE	INCLUDED IN
8 5	FUCHS, Georg	1983	THE ROLE OF SCIENTISTS IN THE PEACE MOVEMENT	PEACE AND THE SCIENCES, NO.1
8 6	FUCHS, George	1985	FOR HUMANKIND THERE IS NO OTHER WAY	PEACE AND THE SCIENCES, NO.1/2
8 7	GALTUNG, Johan	1966	ATTITUDES TOWARDS DIFFERENT FORMS OF DISARMAMENT. A STUDY OF NORWEGIAN PUBLIC OPINION	"PEACE MOVEMENTS & POLITICAL CULTURES", CHATFIELD, C.& DUNGEN, P. (eds.) THE UNIVERSITY TENNESSEE PRESS/ KNOXVILLE
8 8	GALTUNG, Johan	1964	FOREIGN POLICY OPINION AS A FUNCTION OF SOCIAL POSITION	JOURNAL OF PEACE RESEARCH, VOL.1, NO.3-4
8 9	GALTUNG, Johan	1959	PACIFISM FROM A SOCIOLOGICAL POINT OF VIEW	CONFLICT RESOLUTION, VOL.III, NO.I
9 0	GALTUNG, Johan	1986	SCIENTISTS AND THE PEACE MOVEMENT; SOME NOTES ON THE RELATIONSHIP	BULLETIN OF PEACE PROPOSALS, VOL.17, NO.1
9 1	GARSTECKI, Joachim	1984	PEACE WORK WITHIN THE CHURCH IN THE GERMAN DEMOCRATIC REPUBLIC	BULLETIN OF PEACE PROPOSALS, VOL.15, NO.3
9 2	GERLACH, Luther	1983	MOVEMENTS OF REVOLUTIONARY CHANGE; SOME STRUCTURAL CHARACTERISTICS	"SOCIAL MOVEMENTS OF THE SIXTIES AND SEVENTIES", FREEMAN, Jo (ed.) LONGMAN, NEW YORK
9 3	GLEDITSCH, Nils Petter	(in print)	THE RISE AND DECLINE OF THE NEW PEACE MOVEMENTS	"TOWARDS A COMPARATIVE ANALYSIS OF PEACE MOVEMENTS", KODAMA, K. & VESA, U. (eds.) THE DARTMOUTH
9 4	GREPSTAD, Jon	1981	NORWAY AND THE STRUGGLE FOR NUCLEAR DISARMAMENT	A PAPER PREPARED FOR THE 1981 WORLD CONFERENCE AGAINST ATOMIC & HYDROGEN BOMBS, TOKYO-HIROSHIMA-NAGASAKI
9 5	GREPSTAD, Jon	1983	THE PEACE MOVEMENT IN THE NORDIC COUNTRIES	END PAPERS, 4
9 6	GREWE, Hartmut	1985	THE WEST GERMAN PEACE MOVEMENT; A PROFILE	"EUROPEAN PEACE MOVEMENTS & THE FUTURE OF THE WESTERN ALLIANCE", LAQUEUR, W. & HUNTER, R.(eds.) TRANSACTION BOOK, N.J.

	AUTHOR(S)	YEAR	TITLE OF ARTICLE	INCLUDED IN
9 7	GUSFIELD, J. R.	1981	SOCIAL MOVEMENTS AND SOCIAL CHANGE; PERSPECTIVES OF LINEARITY AND FLUIDITY	"RESEARCH IN SOCIAL MOVEMENTS, CONFLICT AND CHANGE", VOL.4, KRIESBERG, L. (ed.) JAI PRESS, GREENWICH & LONDON
9 8	HAAGERUP, Niels Jorgen	1985	THE NORDIC PEACE MOVEMENT	"EUROPEAN PEACE MOVEMENTS & THE FUTURE OF THE WESTERN ALLIANCE", LAQEUR, W. & HUNTER, R.(eds.) TRANSACTION BOOK, N.J.
9 9	HABERMAS, Jürgen	1988	HISTORICAL CONSCIOUSNESS AND POST-TRADITIONAL IDENTITY; REMARKS ON THE FEDERAL REPUBLIC'S ORIENTATION TO THE WEST	ACTA SOCIOLOGICA 31
1 0 0	HABERMAS, Jürgen	1981	NEW SOCIAL MOVEMENT	TELOS, 49, FALL
1 0 1	HALL, B. Welling	1984	THE ANTI-NUCLEAR PEACE MOVEMENT; TOWARD AN EVALUATION OF EFFECTIVENESS	ALTERNATIVES, VOL.IX, NO.4
1 0 2	HALL, B. Welling	1986	THE CHURCH AND THE INDEPENDENT PEACE MOVEMENT IN EASTERN EUROPE	JOURNAL OF PEACE RESEARCH, VOL.23, NO.2
1 0 3	HARASZTI, Miklos	1984	THE HUNGARIAN INDEPENDENT PEACE MOVEMENT	TELOS, 61, FALL
1 0 4	HARLE, Vilho	1985	PEACE RESEARCH AND THE PEACE MOVEMENT	PEACE AND THE SCIENCES, NO.1/2
1 0 5	HARLEY, Anthony	1981	THE REVIVAL OF CND; SOME FACTORS BEHIND RENEWED AGITATION	THE ROUND TABLE, 282
1 0 6	HARTEN, Marten van	1985	PSYCHOLOGICAL PEACEFARE: SOME PROPAGANDA STRATEGIES WITHIN HISTORICAL PEACE TRADITIONS	HISTORISCH VREDES ONDERZOEK, JULY
1 0 7	HEBERLE, Rudolf & GUSFIELD, Joseph R.	1968	SOCIAL MOVEMENT	"INTERNATIONAL ENCYCLOPEDIA OF THE SOCIAL SCIENCES", MACMILLAN & FREEPRESS, NEW YORK
1 0 8	HERF, Jeffrey	1986	WAR, PEACE, AND THE INTELLECTUALS; THE WEST GERMAN PEACE MOVEMENT	INTERNATIONAL SECURITY, 10 (4), SPRING

	AUTHOR(S)	YEAR	TITLE OF ARTICLE	INCLUDED IN
109	HERMON, Elly	1988	THE INTERNATIONAL PEACE EDUCATION MOVEMENT, 1919-1939	"PEACE MOVEMENTS & POLITICAL CULTURES", CHATFIELD, C.& DUNGEN, P. (eds.) THE UNIVERSITY TENNESSEE PRESS/ KNOXVILLE
110	HERNES, Helga M.	1988	SCANDINAVIAN CITIZENSHIP	ACTA SOCIOLOGICA 31, 3
111	HESSE, Dagmar	1985	THE WEST GERMAN PEACE MOVEMENT; A SOCIO-POLITICAL STUDY	MILLENNIUM 14 (1)
112	HIRSCH, Joachim	1982	THE WEST GERMAN PEACE MOVEMENT	TELOS, 51, SPRING
113	HOLL, Karl	1988	GERMAN PACIFISTS IN EXILE, 1933-1940	"PEACE MOVEMENTS & POLITICAL CULTURES", CHATFIELD, C.& DUNGEN, P. (eds.) THE UNIVERSITY TENNESSEE PRESS/ KNOXVILLE
114	HOOK, Glenn D.	(in print)	THE ANTI-NUCLEAR DISCOURSE IN JAPAN; IMPLICATIONS FOR PRAXIS	"TOWARDS A COMPARATIVE ANALYSIS OF PEACE MOVEMENTS", KODAMA, K. & VESA, U. (eds.) DARTMOUTH
115	HUNT, John P.	1985,	SOCIAL POSITION, POLITICAL CONSCIOUSNESS, AND POLITICAL BEHAVIOR; A MULTIVARIATE ANALYSIS, 1968-1972-1976	JOURNAL OF POLITICAL AND MILITARY SOCIOLOGY, 13 (1) SPRING
116	HUNTER, Allen	1988	POST-MARXISM AND THE NEW SOCIAL MOVEMENTS	THEORY AND SOCIETY, 17
117	HUTCHFUL, Eboe	1984	THE PEACE MOVEMENT AND THE THIRD WORLD	ALTERNATIVES, VOL.IX, NO.4
118	HULSBERG, Werner	1985	THE GREENS AT THE CROSSROADS	NEW LEFT REVIEW, JULY-AUGUST
119	INGLEHART, Ronald	1981	POST-MATERIALISM IN AN ENVIRONMENT OF INSECURITY	AMERICAN POLITICAL SCIENCE REVIEW, 75
120	INGLEHART, Ronald	1971	THE SILENT REVOLUTION IN EUROPE; INTERGENERATIONAL CHANGE IN POST-INDUSTRIAL SOCIETIES	THE AMERICAN POLITICAL SCIENCE REVIEW, VOL. 65

	AUTHOR(S)	YEAR	TITLE OF ARTICLE	INCLUDED IN
1 2 1	INGRAM, Norman	1988	ROMAIN ROLLAND, INTERWAR PACIFISM	"PEACE MOVEMENTS & POLITICAL CULTURES", CHATFIELD, C.& DUNGEN, P. (eds.) THE UNIVERSITY TENNESSEE PRESS/ KNOXVILLE
1 2 2	ISERNIA, Pierangelo	1986	PUBLIC OPINION AND PEACE MOBILIZATION	A PAPER PRESENTED AT THE 11TH GENERAL CONFERENCE OF IPRA, UNIVERSITY OF SUSSEX, U.K.
1 2 3	JAHN, Egbert	1984	PROSPECTS AND IMPASSES OF THE NEW PEACE MOVEMENT	BULLETIN OF PEACE PROPOSALS, VOL.15 NO.1
1 2 4	JENKINS, J. Craig	1983	RESOURCE MOBILIZATION THEORY AND THE STUDY OF SOCIAL MOVEMENT	ANNUAL REVIEW OF SOCIOLOGY, VOL.9.
1 2 5	JENKINS, Robin	1967	WHO ARE THESE MARCHERS?	JOURNAL OF PEACE RESEARCH, VOL.4, NO.1
1 2 6	JOSEPHSON, Harold	1988	THE SEARCH FOR LASTING PEACE; INTERNATIONLISM AND AMERICAN FORE:GN POLICY, 1920-1950	"PEACE MOVEMENTS & POLITICAL CULTURES", CHATFIELD, C.& DUNGEN, P. (eds.) THE UNIVERSITY TENNESSEE PRESS/ KNOXVILLE
1 2 7	JOSHUA, Wynfred	1983	SOVIET MANIPULATION OF THE EUROPEAN PEACE MOVEMENT	STRATEGIC REVIEW, WINTER
1 2 8	KALTEFLEITER, Werner	1984	THE GREENS/ALTERNATIVES AND THE PEACE MOVEMENT; A CHALLENGE TO THE GERMAN PARTY SYSTEM	JOURNAL OF PUBLIC AND INTERNATIONAL AFFAIRS, 4 (2) SUMMER
1 2 9	KALTEFLEITER,W. &PFALTZGRAAFF, R.L.	1985	TOWARDS A COMPARATIVE ANALYSIS OF THE PEACE MOVEMENTS	"EUROPEAN PEACE MOVEMENTS & THE FUTURE OF THE WESTERN ALLIANCE", LAQUEUR, W. & HUNTER, R. (eds.) TRANSACTION BOOKS, NJ.
1 3 0	KAY, Susan Ann	1985	FEMINIST IDEOLOGY, RACE, AND (US) POLITICAL PARTICIPATION; A SECOND LOOK	WESTERN POLITICAL QUARTERLY, 38 (3)
1 3 1	KENT, B.	1982	NOTES FROM THE CONCRETE GRASSROOTS	"PROTEST AND SURVIVE", THOMPSON, E.P. & SMITH, D.
1 3 2	KERBO, R.	1982	MOVEMENTS OF "CRISIS" AND MOVEMENTS OF "AFFLUENCE"	JOURNAL OF CONFLICT RESOLUTION, 26, 4

	AUTHOR(S)	YEAR	TITLE OF ARTICLE	INCLUDED IN
133	KITSCHELT, Herbert P.	1986	POLITICAL OPPORTUNITY STRUCTURES AND POLITICAL PROTEST; ANTI-NUCLEAR MOVEMENTS IN FOUR DEMOCRACIES	BRITISH JOURNAL OF POLITICAL SCIENCE 16 (1)
134	KLANDERMANS, Bert	1986	NEW SOCIAL MOVEMENTS AND RESOURCE MOBILIZATION; THE EUROPEAN AND THE AMERICAN APPROACH	INTERNATIONAL JOURNAL OF MASS EMERGENCIES AND DISASTERS, 4
135	KLINEBERG, Otto	1984	PUBLIC OPINION AND NUCLEAR WAR	AMERICAN PSYCHOLOGIST, VOL.39, NO.11
136	KNORR, Lorenz	1985	MASS MOVEMENT AGAINST ATOMIC WAR PLANNING	PEACE AND THE SCIENCES, NO.1/2
137	KODAMA, Katsuya	(in print)	A COMPARATIVE STUDY ON PEACE MOVEMENTS IN JAPAN, DENMARK AND FINLAND	"TOWARDS A COMPARATIVE ANALYSIS OF PEACE MOVEMENTS", KODAMA, K. & VESA, U. (eds.) DARTMOUTH
138	KODAMA, Katsuya	1988	A PARADIGM FOR THE NEW PEACE MOVEMENTS	A PAPER PRESENTED AT 12TH IPRA CONFERENCE IN BRAZIL
139	KODAMA, Katsuya	1987	A STUDY OF THE HIBAKUSHA PEACE MOVEMENTS	BULLETIN OF SOKA PEACE STUDY, NO.7
140	KODAMA, Katsuya	1987	MAJOR STREAMS IN THE JAPANESE PEACE MOVEMENTS	LIFE & PEACE REVIEW, VOL.1, NO. 2
141	KOVALSKY, N.	1982	THE RELIGIOUS COMMUNITY AND THE ANTINUCLEAR MOVEMENT	INTERNATIONAL AFFAIRS, NO.8, AUGUST
142	KRAMER,B.M., KALICK, S.M. & MILBURN, M.A.	1983	ATTITUDES TOWARD NUCLEAR WEAPONS AND NUCLEAR WAR	JOURNAL OF SOCIAL ISSUES, VOL.39. NO.1
143	KRASNER, Michael & PETERSEN, Nikolaj	1986	PEACE AND POLITICS; THE DANISH PEACE MOVEMENT AND ITS IMPACT ON NATIONAL SECURITY POLICY	JOURNAL OF PEACE RESEARCH, VOL.23, NO.2
144	KRASNER, Michael A.	(in print)	DECLINE AND PERSISTENCE IN THE CONTEMPORARY DANISH AND BRITISH PEACE MOVEMENTS; A COMPARATIVE ANALYSIS	"TOWARDS A COMPARATIVE ANALYSIS OF PEACE MOVEMENTS", KODAMA, K. & VESA, U. (eds.) DARTMOUTH

	AUTHOR(S)	YEAR	TITLE OF ARTICLE	INCLUDED IN
145	KRIESI, Hanspeter	1989	NEW SOCIAL MOVEMENTS AND THE NEW CLASS IN THE NETHERLANDS	AJS VOL. 94 NO.5
146	KRIESI, Hanspeter & PRAAG, Philip van, Jr.	1987	OLD AND NEW POLITICS; THE DUTCH PEACE MOVEMENT AND THE TRADITIONAL POLITICAL ORGANIZATIONS	EUROPEAN JOURNAL FOR POLITICAL SCIENCE 15
147	KURINO, Ohtori & KODAMA, Katsuya	(in print)	A STUDY ON THE JAPANESE PEACE MOVEMENT	"TOWARDS A COMPARATIVE ANALYSIS OF PEACE MOVEMENTS", KODAMA, K. & VESA, U. (eds.) DARTMOUTH
148	KÖSZEGI, Ferenc & SZENT-IVANYI, Istvan	1983	THE PEACE MOVEMENT IN EASTERN EUROPE	PRAXIS INTERNATIONAL, VOL.3, NO.1
149	KÖSZEGI, Ferenc & THOMPSON, E.P.	1982	THE NEW HUNGARIAN PEACE MOVEMENT	END SPECIAL REPORT
150	LADD, E.C.Jr.	1979	PURSUING THE NEW CLASS; SOCIAL THEORY AND SURVEY DATA	"NEW CLASS", BRUCE-BRIGGS, B. (ed.) TRANSACTION, NEW BRUNSWICK, N.J.
151	LADD, E.C.Jr.	1978	THE NEW LINES ARE DRAWN	PUBLIC OPINION, 1
152	LAITINEN, A.	1984	MARATHON PEACE MARCH: A DEMONSTRATION OF INTERNATIONAL UNDERSTANDING	"SPORT AND INTERNATIONAL UNDERSTANDING" ILMARINEN, Teoksessa M. (ed.)
153	LANGILLE, David	1986	THE PEACE MOVEMENT, PARTIES AND POLITICAL POWER	A PAPER PRESENTED AT THE 11TH GENERAL CONFERENCE OF IPRA, UNIVERSITY OF SUSSEX, U.K.
154	LINDBERG, Steve	1982	THE ILLUSORY NORDIC BALANCE; THREAT SCENARIOS IN NORDIC SECURITY PLANNING	COOPERATION AND CONFLICT, VOL.17. NO.1
155	LINDKVIST, Kent	(in print)	MOBILIZATION PEAKS AND DECLINES OF THE SWEDISH PEACE MOVEMENT	"TOWARDS A COMPARATIVE ANALYSIS OF PEACE MOVEMENTS", KODAMA, K. & VESA, U. (eds.) DARTMOUTH
156	LODGAARD, Sverre	1980	A NWFZ IN THE NORTH?	BULLETIN OF PEACE PROPOSALS, VOL.11, NO.1

	AUTHOR(S)	YEAR	TITLE OF ARTICLE	INCLUDED IN
157	LOKSHIN, Grigori	1985	THE PRESENT PEACE MOVEMENT - PROBLEMS AND PREJUDICES	PEACE AND THE SCIENCES, NO.1/2
158	LUBELSKI-BERNARD, Nadine	1988	FREEMASONRY AND PEACE IN EUROPE, 1867-1914	"PEACE MOVEMENTS & POLITICAL CULTURES", CHATFIELD, C.& DUNGEN, P. (eds.) THE UNIVERSITY TENNESSEE PRESS/ KNOXVLLE
159	LUMSDEN, Malhem	1983	NUCLEAR WEAPONS AND THE NEW PEACE MOVEMENT	"SIPRI YEAR BOOK 1983", SIPRI
160	LÖE, Håkan	1982	THE NORDIC COUNTRIES AND THE QUESTION OF NUCLEAR DISARMAMENT: THE NUCLEAR FREE ZONE MOVEMENTS	A PAPER SUBMITTED TO THE 12TH IPSA WORLD CONGRESS, RIO DE JANEIRO
161	MAGRI, Lucio	1982	THE PEACE MOVEMENT AND EUROPEAN SOCIALISM	NEW LEFT REVIEW, NO.131
162	MARTIN, Brian	1982	HOW THE PEACE MOVEMENT SHOULD BE PREPARING FOR NUCLEAR WAR	BULLETIN OF PEACE PROPOSALS, VOL.13, NO.2
163	MATTAUSCH, John	1987	THE SOCIOLOGY OF CND	"THE SOCIOLOGY OF WAR AND PEACE", CREIGHTON, C. & SHAW, M. (eds.) MACMILLAN PRESS, LONDON
164	MAUD, George	1982	THE FURTHER SHORES OF FINLANDIZATION	COOPERATION AND CONFLICT, VOL.17, NO.1
165	MCADAM, John	1987	TESTING THE THEORY OF THE NEW CLASS	SOCIOLOGICAL QUARTERLY, 28
166	MELUCCI, Alberto	1984	AN END TO SOCIAL MOVEMENT?	SOCIAL SCIENCE INFORMATION, VOL.24
167	MELUCCI, Alberto	1985	THE SYMBOLIC CHALLENGES OF CONTEMPORARY MOVEMENTS	SOCIAL RESEARCH, VOL.52, NO.4
168	MILBRAATH, Lester W.	1981	POLITICAL PARTICIPATION	"THE HANDBOOK OF POLITICAL BEHAVIOR, VOL.4", LONG, S.L. (ed.), PLENUM, NEW YORK

	AUTHOR(S)	YEAR	TITLE OF ARTICLE	INCLUDED IN
169	MILLER, B. Jaye	1984	THE NUCLEAR EXPERIENCE; JAPAN'S UNKNOWN PEACE MOVEMENT	SOCIALIST REVIEW, 14 (6)
170	MUSHABEN, Joyce Marie	1985	CYCLES OF PEACE PROTEST IN WEST GERMANY; EXPERIENCES FROM THREE DECADES	WEST EUROPEAN POLITICS, VOL.8, NO.1
171	MUSHABEN, Joyce Marie	1986	GRASSROOTS AND GEWALTFREIE AKTIONEN: A STUDY OF MASS MOBILIZAITON STRATEGIES IN THE WEST GERMAN PEACE MOVEMENT	JOURNAL OF PEACE RESEARCH, VOL.23, NO.2
172	MUSHABEN, Joyce Marie	1984	SWORDS TO PLOWSHARES; THE CHURCH, THE STATE AND THE EAST GERMAN PEACE MOVEMENT	STUDIES IN COMPARATIVE COMMUNISM, 17 (2)
173	MYERS, Frank E.	1973	DILENMMAS IN THE BRITISH PEACE MOVEMENT SINCE WORLD WAR II	JOURNAL OF PEACE RESEARCH, VOL.10, NO.1-2
174	MYERS, Susan E.	(in print)	SETTING THE RESEARCH AGENDA: A PROPOSAL TO STUDY NON-GOVERNMENTAL RELIGIOUS ORGANIZATIONS' INFLUENCE ON U.S. NUCLEAR WEAPONS POLICY	"TOWARDS A COMPARATIVE ANALYSIS OF PEACE MOVEMENTS", KODAMA, K. & VESA, U. (eds.) DARTMOUTH
175	MÜLLER-ROMMERL, Ferdinand	1985	NEW SOCIAL MOVEMENTS AND SMALLER PARTIES; A COMPARATIVE PERSPECTIVE	WEST EUROPEAN POLITICS, VOL.8, NO.1
176	MÜLLER-ROMMERL, Ferdinand	1985	SOCIAL MOVEMENTS AND THE GREENS; NEW INTERNAL POLITICS IN GERMANY	EUROPEAN JOURNAL OF POLITICAL RESEARCH, 13 (1)
177	NEDELMANN, Birgitta	1984	NEW POLITICAL MOVEMENTS AND CHANGES IN PROCESSES OF INTERMEDIAT:ON	SOCIAL SCIENCE INFORMATION, VOL.23, NO.6
178	NILSON, Sten Sparre	1985	THE PEACE MOVEMENT IN NORWAY	"EUROPEAN PEACE MOVEMENTS & THE FUTURE OF THE WESTERN ALLIANCE", LAQUEUR, W. & HUNTER, R. (eds.) TRANSACTION BOOK, N.J.
179	OFFE, Claus	1985	NEW SOCIAL MOVEMENTS: CHALLENGING THE BOUNDARIES OF INSTITUTIONAL POLITICS	SOCIAL RESEARCH, (WINTER)
180	OHNISHI, Hitoshi	1983	PEACE MOVEMENT IN JAPAN	INTERNATIONAL PEACE RESEARCH NEWSLETTER, VOL.XXI, NO.3

	AUTHOR(S)	YEAR	TITLE OF ARTICLE	INCLUDED IN
181	OLOFSSON, Gunnar	1988	AFTER THE WORKING-CLASS MOVEMENT? AN ESSAY ON WHAT'S 'NEW' AND WHAT'S 'SOCIAL' IN THE NEW SOCIAL MOVEMENTS	ACTA SOCIOLOGICA 31, 1
182	OPP, Karl-Dieter	1986	SOFT INCENTIVES AND COLLECTIVE ACTION; PARTICIPATION IN THE ANTI-NUCLEAR MOVEMENT	POLITICAL SCIENCE, 16 (1)
183	ORMROD, David	1987	THE CHURCHES AND THE NUCLEAR ARMS RACE, 1945-85	"CAMPAIGN FOR PEACE;BRITISH PEACE MOVEMENTS IN THE TWENTIETH CENTURY" TAYLOR, R.& YOUNG,N.(eds.)MANCHESTER UNIV. PRESS
184	PATTERSON, David S.	1988	CITIZEN PEACE INITIATIVES AND AMERICAN POLITICAL CULTURE, 1865-1920	"PEACE MOVEMENTS & POLITICAL CULTURES", CHATFIELD, C.& DUNGEN, P. (eds.) THE UNIVERSITY TENNESSEE PRESS/ KNOXVILLE
185	PETERSEN, Nikolaj	1985	THE SCANDILUX EXPERIMENT; TOWARDS A TRANSNATIONAL SOCIAL DEMOCRATIC SECURITY PERSPECTIVE?	COOPERATION AND CONFLICT, VOL.20, NO.1
186	PIETILÄ, Hilkka	1984	WOMEN'S PEACE MOVEMENT AS AN INNOVATIVE PROPONENT OF THE PEACE MOVEMENT AS A WHOLE	IFDA DOSSIER, 43 SEPTEMBER/OCTOBER
187	POTTER, Paul	1966	THE INTELLECTUAL AND SOCIAL CHANGE	"THE NEW STUDENT LEFT", COHEN, M.& HALE, D. (eds.) BEACON PRESS, BOSTON
188	RAMET, Pedro	1984	THE CHURCH AND PEACE IN THE GDR	PROBLEMS OF COMMUNISM, VOL.33
189	RANDLE, Michael	1987	NON-VIOLENT DIRECT ACTION IN THE 1950S AND 1960S	"CAMPAIGN FOR PEACE;BRITISH PEACE MOVEMENTS IN THE TWENTIETH CENTURY" TAYLOR, R.& YOUNG,N.(eds.)MANCHESTER UNIV. PRESS
190	RAPOPORT, Anatol	1983	PEACE RESEARCH AND PEACE MOVEMENTS	INTERNATIONAL PEACE RESEARCH NEWSLETTER, VOL.XXI, NO.3
191	REEADER, Mark	1984	THE BRITISH PEACE MOVEMENT IN THE 1980s	PEACE AND CHANGE, 9 (4)
192	RIDGEWAY, James	1983	THE FREEZE MOVEMENT VERSUS REAGAN	NEW LEFT REVIEW, NO.137 JAN.-FEB.

	AUTHOR(S)	YEAR	TITLE OF ARTICLE	INCLUDED IN
193	RIGBY, Andrew & CLARK, Howard	1982	NO EUROSHIMAS; THE NUCLEAR DISARMAMENT CHAMPAIGN IN EUROPE	GANDHI MARG, VOL.4: 2-3
194	ROBERTS, Carl W.; LANG, Kurt	1985	GENERATIONS AND IDEOLOGICAL CHANGE; SOME OBSERVATIONS	PUBLIC OPINION QUARTERLY, 49 (4)
195	ROBINSON, Wayne	1983	PEACE RESEARCH AND ACTIVISM IN NEW ZEALAND	INTERNATIONAL PEACE RESEARCH NEWSLETTER, VOL.XXI, NO.3
196	ROSSI, Sergio A. & ILARI, Virgilio	1985	THE PEACE MOVEMENT IN ITALY	"EUROPEAN PEACE MOVEMENTS & THE FUTURE OF THE WESTERN ALLIANCE", LAQUEUR, W.& HUNTER, R. (eds.) TRANSACTION BOOKS, N.J.
197	RUGE, Mari Holmboe	1966	ARE YOU A MEMBER OF A PEACE ORDGANIZATION?	JOURNAL OF PEACE RESEARCH, VOL.3, NO.4
198	RUPPRECHT, Frank	(in print)	PEACE MOVEMENT IN HISTORY AND AT PRESENT	"TOWARDS A COMPARATIVE ANALYSIS OF PEACE MOVEMENTS", KODAMA, K. & VESA, U. (eds.) DARTMOUTH
199	SALOMON, Kim	1986	THE PEACE MOVEMENT - AN ANTI-ESTABLISHMENT MOVEMENT	JOURNAL OF PEACE RESEARCH, VOL.23, NO.2
200	SARACINO, Maria Antonietta	1988	WOMAN, THE UNWILLING VICTIM OF WAR; THE LEGACY OF OLIVE SCHREINER (1855-1920)	"PEACE MOVEMENTS & POLITICAL CULTURES", CHATFIELD, C.& DUNGEN, P. (eds.) THE UNIVERSITY TENNESSEE PRESS/ KNOXVILLE
201	SCASE, Richard	1983	WHY SWEDEN HAS ELECTED A RADICAL GOVERNMENT	POLITICAL QUARTERLY, 54 (1) JAN.-MARCH
202	SCHLAGA, Rüdiger	(in print)	PEACE MOVEMENT AS A PARTY'S TOOL? THE PEACE COUNCIL OF THE GERMAN DEMOCRATIC REPUBLIC	"TOWARDS A COMPARATIVE ANALYSIS OF PEACE MOVEMENTS", KODAMA, K. & VESA, U. (eds.) DARTMOUTH
203	SCHMID, Herman	1966	ON A STUDY OF A SWEDISH PEACE ORGANIZATION	A PAPER PRESENTED AT THE SECOND NORDIC CONFERENCE ON PEACE RESEARCH, HILLERÖD, DENMARK
204	SCHNEIDER, H.	1984	PEACE MOVEMENTS IN EUROPE	"ENERGY AND SECURITY CONCERNS IN THE ATLANTIC COMMUNITY", FELD, W.J. (ed.)

	AUTHOR(S)	YEAR	TITLE OF ARTICLE	INCLUDED IN
205	SEGBERS, Klaus	1982	THE EUROPEAN PEACE MOVEMENT, THE SOVIET UNION, AND THE AMERICAN LEFT	TELOS, 54, WINTER
206	SHARP, Gene	1980	MAKING THE ABOLITION OF WAR A REALISTIC GOAL	"ALTERNATIVE METHODS FOR INTERNATIONAL SECURITY", STEPHENSON, C.M. (ed.)
207	SHARP, Gene	1959	THE MEANINGS OF NON-VIOLENCE: A TYPOLOGY (REVISED)	CONFLICT RESOLUTION, VOL.III, NO.1
208	SHAW, Martin	1987	WAR, PEACE AND BRITISH MARXISM, 1895-1945	"CAMPAIGN FOR PEACE;BRITISH PEACE MOVE-MENTS IN THE TWENTIETH CENTURY" TAYLOR, R.& YOUNG,N.(eds.)MANCHESTER UNIV. PRESS
209	SHERRY, N. H.	1985	THE PEACE MOVEMENT IN THE NETHERLANDS	"EUROPEAN PEACE MOVEMENTS & THE FUTURE OF THE WESTERN ALLIANCE", LAQUEUR, W. & HUNTER, R. (eds.) TRANSACTION BOOK, N.J.
210	SHIPLEY, Peter	1986	PATTERNS OF PROTEST IN WESTERN EUROPE	CONFLICT STUDIES, 189
211	SIMON, Werners	1988	THE INTERNATIONAL PEACE BUREAU, 1892-1917; CLERK, MEDIATOR, OR GUIDE?	"PEACE MOVEMENTS & POLITICAL CULTURES", CHATFIELD, C.& DUNGEN, P. (eds.) THE UNIVERSITY TENNESSEE PRESS/ KNOXVILLE
212	SKELLY , James M.	1988	POWER/KNOWLEDGE: THE PROBLEMS OF PEACE RESEARCH AND THE PEACE MOVEMENT	"A JUST PEACE THROUGH TRANSFORMATION" ALGER, Chadwick & STOHL, Michael (eds.) WESTVIEW PRESS, BOULDER & LONDON
213	SMALL, Melvin	1984	THE IMPACT OF THE ANTIWAR MOVEMENT ON LYNDON JOHANSON, 1965-1968; A PRELIMINARY REPORT	PEACE AND CHANGE, 10 (1)
214	SMELSER, Neil	1968	SOCIAL PSYCHOLOGICAL DIMENTIONS OF COLLECTIVE BEHAVIOR	"ESSAYS IN SOCIOLOGICAL EXPLANATION", SMELSER, Neil (ed.)
215	SMET, Luc De	(in print)	THE BELGIAN PEACE MOVEMENT POLLED	"TOWARDS A COMPARATIVE ANALYSIS OF PEACE MOVEMENTS", KODAMA, K. & VESA, U. (eds.) DARTMOUTH
216	STEINKE, R.	1982	IS THE PEACE MOVEMENT A SINGLE ISSUE MOVEMENT?	END PAPERS 3, AUTUMN

	AUTHOR(S)	YEAR	TITLE OF ARTICLE	INCLUDED IN
2 1 7	STRONG, Robert A.	1983	NUCLEAR PROTEST IN BRITAIN AND AMERICA	ARMS CONTROL 4 (2)
2 1 8	SUMMY, Ralph	1988	THE AUSTRALIAN PEACE COUNCIL AND THE ANTICOMMUNIST MILIEW, 1949-1965	"PEACE MOVEMENTS & POLITICAL CULTURES", CHATFIELD, C.& DUNGEN, P. (eds.) THE UNIVERSITY TENNESSEE PRESS/ KNOXVILLE
2 1 9	SWIDEREK, Stanislaw	1985	SOME REMARKS ON THE HISTORICAL EXPERIENCES OF THE PEACE MOVEMENT IN WESTERN EUROPE	PEACE AND THE SCIENCES, NO.1/2
2 2 0	SZELENYI, Ivan & MARTIN, Bill	1988	THE THREE WAVES OF NEW CLASS THEORIES	THEORY AND SOCIETY, 17
2 2 1	TAAGEPERA, Rein	1986	CITIZENS' PEACE MOVEMENT IN THE SOVIET BALTIC REPUBLIC	JOURNAL OF PEACE RESEARCH, VOL.23, NO.2
2 2 2	TAAGEPERA, Rein	1985	INCLUSION OF BALTIC REPUBLICS IN THE NORDIC NUCLEAR-FREE ZONE	JOURNAL OF BALTIC STUDIES, VOL.16. NO.1
2 2 3	TAAGEPERA, Rein	1986	PEACE MOVEMENT IN THE SOVIET BALTIC REPUBLIC	JOURNAL OF PEACE RESEARCH, VOL.23, NO.2
2 2 4	TAYLOR, Richard	1983	THE BRITISH PEACE MOVEMENT AND SOCIALIST CHANGE	THE SOCIALIST REGISTER
2 2 5	TAYLOR, Richard	1987	THE LABOUR PARTY AND CND; 1957-1984	"CAMPAIGN FOR PEACE;BRITISH PEACE MOVE-MENTS IN THE TWENTIETH CENTURY" TAYLOR, R.& YOUNG,N.(eds.)MANCHESTER UNIV. PRESS
2 2 6	TAYLOR, Richard	1987	THE MARXIST LEFT AND THE PEACE MOVEMENT IN BRITAIN SINCE 1945	"CAMPAIGN FOR PEACE;BRITISH PEACE MOVE-MENTS IN THE TWENTIETH CENTURY" TAYLOR, R.& YOUNG,N.(eds.)MANCHESTER UNIV. PRESS
2 2 7	TAYLOR, Richard & YOUNG, Nigel	1987	BRITAIN AND THE INTERNATIONAL PEACE MOVEMENT IN THE 1989S	"CAMPAIGN FOR PEACE;BRITISH PEACE MOVE-MENTS IN THE TWENTIETH CENTURY" TAYLOR, R.& YOUNG,N. (eds.) MANCHESTER UNIV. PRESS
2 2 8	THIBAUD, Paul	1984	PACIFISM AND ITS PROBLEMS	TELOS, 59, SPRING

	AUTHOR(S)	YEAR	TITLE OF ARTICLE	INCLUDED IN
229	THIELEMANN, Dieter	1985	THE PEACE MOVEMENT AND THE SOVIET AMERICAN NEGOTIATIONS ON NUCLEAR AND SPACE WEAPONS REQUIREMENTS	PEACE AND THE SCIENCES, NO.1/2
230	TILLY, Charles	1985	MODELS AND REALITIES OF POPULAR COLLECTIVE ACTION	SOCIAL RESEARCH, VOL.52, NO.4
231	TIMOFEEV, Timur	1985	TRENDS IN THE ANTI-NUCLEAR MOVEMENT- SOME SOCIAL ASPECTS	PEACE AND THE SCIENCES, NO.1/2
232	TOMEK, Ivan & HERZMANN, Jan	(in print)	SOME QUESTIONS CONCERNING PEACE AND WAR IN PUBLIC OPINION IN THE CSSR	"TOWARDS A COMPARATIVE ANALYSIS OF PEACE MOVEMENTS", KODAMA, K. & VESA, U. (eds.) DARTMOUTH
233	TOURAINE, Alain	1985	AN INTRODUCTION TO THE STUDY OF SOCIAL MOVEMENTS	SOCIAL RESEARCH, VOL.52, NO.4
234	TYLER, Tom R. & MCGRAW, Kathleen M.	1983	THE THREAT OF NUCLEAR WAR; RISK INTERPRETATION AND BEHAVIORAL RESPONSE	JOURNAL OF SOCIAL ISSUES, VOL.39, NO.1
235	VÆRNØ, Grethe	1983	A PUBLIC OPINION STRATEGY	NATO REVIEW, NO.3-4
236	VEER, Ben ter	1983	NEW PEACE MOVEMENT IN WESTERN EUROPE	INTERNATIONAL PEACE RESEARCH NEWSLETTER, VOL.XXI, NO.3
237	VELLACOTT, Jo	1988	WOMEN, PEACE, AND INTERNATIONALISM, 1914-1920	"PEACE MOVEMENTS & POLITICAL CULTURES", CHATFIELD, C.& DUNGEN, P. (eds.) THE UNIVERSITY TENNESSEE PRESS/ KNOXVILLE
238	VERMAAT, J.A. Emerson	1985	THE STRANGE PHENOMENON OF THE "GENERALS FOR PEACE"	STRATEGIC REVIEW, 13 (2)
239	VERMAAT, J.A. Emerson	1982	MOSCOW FRONTS AND THE EUROPEAN PEACE MOVEMENT	PROBLEMS OF COMMUNISM, VOL.31 (6)
240	VESA, Unto	(in print)	PEACE MOVEMENT AND PUBLIC OPINION IN FINLAND	"TOWARDS A COMPARATIVE ANALYSIS OF PEACE MOVEMENTS", KODAMA, K. & VESA, U. (eds.) DARTMOUTH

	AUTHOR(S)	YEAR	TITLE OF ARTICLE	INCLUDED IN
2 4 1	VOLMERG, Ute	1984	FOLIE A DEUX: PEACE MOVEMENT AND DETERRENCE EXPERTS ON THEIR WAY TO THE ABYSS?	BULLETIN OF PEACE PROPOSALS, VOL.15, NO.1
2 4 2	VOORST, L.Bruce van	1982	THE CRITICAL MASSES	FOREIGN POLICY, NO.48
2 4 3	WÆVER, Ole	(in print)	POLITICS OF MOVEMENT; A CONTRIBUTION TO POLITICAL THEORY ON AND IN PEACE MOVEMENTS	"TOWARDS A COMPARATIVE ANALYSIS OF PEACE MOVEMENTS", KODAMA, K. & VESA, U. (eds.) DARTMOUTH
2 4 4	WALSH, Edward J.& WARLAND, Rex H.	1983	SOCIAL MOVEMENT INVOLVEMENT IN THE WAKE OF A NUCLEAR ACCIDENT: ACTIVISTS AND FREE RIDERS IN THE TMI AREA	AMERICAN SOCIOLOGICAL REVIEW, 48 (6) DEC.
2 4 5	WANK, Solomon	1988	THE AUSTRIAN PEACE MOVEMENT AND THE HABSBURG RULING ELITE, 1906-1914	"PEACE MOVEMENTS & POLITICAL CULTURES", CHATFIELD, C.& DUNGEN, P. (eds.) THE UNIVERSITY TENNESSEE PRESS/ KNOXVILLE
2 4 6	WASMUHT, Ulrike	1983	A NEW STRUGGLE FOR PEACE: A SOCIOLOGICAL ANALYSIS OF NORTH-AMERICAN PEACE CLUSTERS	A PAPER PRESENTED AT THE 10TH GENERAL CONFERENCE OF IPRA, GYÖR, HUNGARY
2 4 7	WASMUHT, Ulrike	1984	A SOCIOLOGICAL SURVEY OF AMERICAN PEACE MOVEMENTS	ALTERNATIVES, VOL.IX, NO.4.
2 4 8	WASMUHT, Ulrike	1985	TOWARDS AN ANALYSIS OF THE PEACE MOVEMENT IN THE FEDERAL REPUBLIC OF GERMANY	PEACE AND THE SCIENCES, NO.1/2
2 4 9	WEHR, Paul	1986	NUCLEAR PACIFISM AS COLLECTIVE ACTION	JOURNAL OF PEACE RESEARCH, VOL.23, NO.2
2 5 0	WEILER, Rudolf	1985	PEACE MOVEMENTS, DEVELOPMENT, STATE OF AFFAIRS. DEFINITION	PEACE AND THE SCIENCES, NO.1/2
2 5 1	WEILER, Rudolf	1983	THE COMPETENCE OF PEACE MOVEMENTS	PEACE AND THE SCIENCES, NO.1
2 5 2	WETTIG, Gerhard	1984	THE WESTERN PEACE MOVEMENT IN MOSCOW'S LONGER VIEW	STRATEGIC REVIEW, 12 (2)

	AUTHOR(S)	YEAR	TITLE OF ARTICLE	INCLUDED IN
2 5 3	WIELAND, Oeba	1985	PEACE MOVEMENTS: AN IMPORTANT FACTOR IN PUBLIC LIFE	PEACE AND THE SCIENCES, NO.1/2
2 5 4	WITTNER, Lawrence S.	1988	THE TRANSNATIONAL MOVEMENT AGAINST NUCLEAR WEAPONS, 1945-1986; A PRELIMINARY SURVEY	"PEACE MOVEMENTS & POLITICAL CULTURES", CHATFIELD, C.& DUNGEN, P. (eds.) THE UNIVERSITY TENNESSEE PRESS/ KNOXVILLE
2 5 5	WOLFE, Alan	1983	WHY IS THERE NO GREEN PARTY IN THE UNITED STATES?	WORLD POLICY JOURNAL, 1 (1) FALL
2 5 6	WOODWARD, Beverly	1980	NONVIOLENT STRUGGLE, NONVIOLENT DEFENSE, AND NONVIOLENT PEACE MAKING	"ALTERNATIVE METHODS FOR INTERNATIONAL SECURITY", STEPHENSON, C.M.(ed.)
2 5 7	YOST, David S. & GLAD, Thomas C.	1982	WEST GERMAN PARTY POLITICS AND THEATER NUCLEAR MODERNIZATION SINCE 1977	ARMED FORCES AND SOCIETY, VOL.8, NO.4, SUMMER
2 5 8	YOUNG, Nigel	1982	AVERTING HOLOCAUST, STRATEGIES FOR POPULAR INTERVENTION AND INITIATIVE IN THE THERMONUCLEAR AGE	"THE NUCLEAR ARMS AGE" BARNABY, Frank & THOMAS, G.P. (eds.) FRANCES PINTER, LONDON
2 5 9	YOUNG, Nigel	1981	EDUCATING THE PEACE EDUCATORS	BULLETIN OF PEACE PROPOSALS, VOL.12, NO.2
2 6 0	YOUNG, Nigel	1983	NEW STRATEGIES FOR DISARMAMENT: PERSPECTIVES FOR PEACE ACTION AND THE ROLE OF THE PEACE TRADITIONS	PRIO PAPER, 5/83
2 6 1	YOUNG, Nigel	1977	NONVIOLENCE AND SOCIAL CHANGE	NEW INTERNATIONALIST, MARCH
2 6 2	YOUNG, Nigel	(in print)	ON THE STUDY OF PEACE MOVEMENTS; INTRODUCTORY PRESENTATION	"TOWARDS A COMPARATIVE ANALYSIS OF PEACE MOVEMENTS", KODAMA, K. & VESA, U. (eds.) THE DARTMOUTH
2 6 3	YOUNG, Nigel	1987	PEACE MOVEMENTS IN HISTORY	"TOWARDS A JUST WORLD PEACE", MENDLOVITZ, Saul H. and WALKER, R.B.J.(eds.) BUTTERWORTHS, LONDON
2 6 4	YOUNG, Nigel	1983	SENSING THEIR STRENGTH; TOWARDS A POLITICAL STRATEGY FOR THE NEW PEACE MOVEMENTS IN EUROPE	BULLETIN OF PEACE PROPOSALS, VOL.14, NO.2.

	AUTHOR(S)	YEAR	TITLE OF ARTICLE	INCLUDED IN
265	YOUNG, Nigel	1984	SOME CURRENT CONTROVERSIES IN THE NEW PEACE EDUCATION MOVEMENT	BULLETIN OF PEACE PROPOSALS, VOL.15, NO.2
266	YOUNG, Nigel	1983	STRATEGIES OF THE NEW PEACE MOVEMENT	PRIO PAPER, 5/83
267	YOUNG, Nigel	1983	THAT WAS THE WEEK THAT WAS - ALMOST OUR LAST	"THE CND STORY", MINNION, John. & BOLSOVR, Philip. (eds.) ALLISON & BUSBY, LONDON
268	YOUNG, Nigel	1983	THE CONTEMPORARY EUROPEAN ANTI-NUCLEAR EXPERIMENTS IN THE MOBILIZATION OF PUBLIC POWER	PRIO PAPER, 3/83
269	YOUNG, Nigel	1987	THE CONTEMPORARY EUROPEAN ANTI-NUCLEAR MOVEMENT	"THE ARMS RACE AND NUCLEAR WAR", EVAN, Willian M. & HILGARTNER, Stephan (eds.) PRENTICE HALL, ENGLEWOOD
270	YOUNG, Nigel	1983	THE CONTEMPORARY PEACE EDUCATION MOVEMENT	PRIO PAPER, 6/83
271	YOUNG, Nigel	1983	THE CUBA CRISIS AND CND	"THE CND STORY", MINNION, John. & BOLSOVR, Philip. (eds.)
272	YOUNG, Nigel	1977	THE NEW LEFT REVISITED	NEW SOCIETY, SEPT.
273	YOUNG, Nigel	1983	THE NEW PEACE EDUCATION MOVEMENT	PERSPECTIVES, VOL.1, NO.1
274	YOUNG, Nigel	1987	THE PEACE MOVEMENT AND PERSPECTIVES FOR PEACE	BULLETIN OF PEACE PROPOSALS, A SPECIAL ISSUE
275	YOUNG, Nigel	1985	THE PEACE MOVEMENT IN BRITAIN	PRIO PAPER, 7/85
276	YOUNG, Nigel	1987	THE PEACE MOVEMENT, PEACE RESEARCH, PEACE EDUCATION AND PEACE BUILDING	BULLETIN OF PEACE PROPOSALS, VOL.18, NO.3

	AUTHOR(S)	YEAR	TITLE OF ARTICLE	INCLUDED IN
277	YOUNG, Nigel	1986	THE PEACE MOVEMENT: A COMPARATIVE AND ANALYTICAL SURVEY	ALTERNATIVES, VOL.XI
278	YOUNG, Nigel	1961	THE POLITICAL VIRGINS	NEW UNIVERSITY
279	YOUNG, Nigel	1981	THE STATE FRAMEWORK OF PEACE EDUCATION	BULLETIN OF PEACE PROPOSALS, VOL.12, NO.2
280	YOUNG, Nigel	1987	TRADITION AND INNOVATION IN THE BRITISH PEACE MOVEMENT; TOWARDS AN ANALYTICAL FRAMEWORK	"CAMPAIGN FOR PEACE;BRITISH PEACE MOVE-MENTS IN THE TWENTIETH CENTURY" TAYLOR, R.& YOUNG,N.(eds.)MANCHESTER UNIV. PRESS
281	YOUNG, Nigel	1983	TRANSNATIONALISM AND WAR RESISTANCE	GANDHI MARG, JULY
282	YOUNG, Nigel	1987	WAR RESISTANCE AND THE BRITISH MARXISM, 1895-1945	"CAMPAIGN FOR PEACE;BRITISH PEACE MOVE-MENTS IN THE TWENTIETH CENTURY" TAYLOR, R.& YOUNG,N.(eds.)MANCHESTER UNIV. PRESS
283	YOUNG, Nigel	1984	WAR RESISTANCE, STATE AND SOCIETY	"WAR, STATE AND SOCIETY", SHAW, M. (ed.) MACMILLAN, LONDON
284	YOUNG, Nigel	1983	WHY DO PEACE MOVEMENTS FAIL?; AN HISTORICAL AND SOCIAL OVERVIEW	PRIO WORKING PAPER, 10/83
285	ZALD, Mayer & ASH, Roberta	1966	SOCIAL MOVEMENTS; GROWTH, DECAY AND CHANGE	SOCIAL FORCES, VOL.44
286	ZALD, Mayer N.	1987	THE FUTURE OF SOCIAL MOVEMENTS	"SOCIAL MOVEMENTS IN AN ORGANIZATIONAL SOCIETY", ZALD,M.N.& MCCARTHY, J.D. (eds.) TRANSACTION, NEW BRUNSWICK, N.J.
287	ZAMOSHKIN, Yuri	1984	CHRISTIAN CHURCHES AND THE MODERN PEACE MOVEMENT	PEACE AND THE SCIENCES, NO.4

About the authors

Jan Øberg
Dr., director of Lund University Peace Research Institute (LUPRI) and of the Transnational Foundation for Peace and Future Research (TFF), in Lund.

Chadwick F. Alger
Professor of political science, Ohio State University, Secretary-General of IPRA between 1983 and 1986, co-editor with Michael Stohl of *A Just Peace Through Transformation,* Westview Press 1988.

Radmila Nakarada
Dr., senior-fellow, Institute for International Labour Movements in Belgrade, member of the advisory board of TFF in Lund, and co-editor of *Surviving Together. The Olof Palme Lectures on Common Security 1988*, Dartmouth 1989.

Shingo Shibata
Professor, Faculty of Integrated Arts and Sciences, Hiroshima University.
Shibata is the author of several books, including *Lessons of the Vitenam War* (Amsterdam, 1973) and *Revolution in der Philosophie* (Westberlin 1977). He has organized peace music concerts in August every year since 1980 to commemorate the victims of Hiroshima and Nagasaki.

Paul Smoker
Ph.D., professor, Richardson Institute for Peace Studies, Lancaster University, presently editor of IPRA Newsletter, a prolific writer on a wide variety of peace research subjects through decades.

Katsuya Kodama
Guest researcher at LUPRI. Co-convenor of IPRA's study group on peace movements. Co-editor of *Towards a Comparative Analysis of Peace Movements,* Dartmouth Publishing Company 1989 (in print) and author of *Life Histories of Atomic Bomb Orphans* (in Japanese), The Choubunsha, 1987. Kodama is finalizing his Ph.D. dissertation on the Swedish peace movements.

The IPRA study group
on peace movements

Background
The Study Group on Peace Movements was established at the general conference of the International Peace Research Association in Györ, Hungary, in 1983. Nigel Young became convenor of the group for the first years and is now co-convenor with Katsuya Kodama. Five meetings have been organized. The first meeting was held at the IUC in Dubrovnik, Yugoslavia, in April, 1985. The second meeting was held in Elsinore, Denmark in August, 1985 and the third was held during the IPRA General Conference in Sussex, April 1986.

The study group arranged a conference under the general theme of "Towards a Comparative Analysis of Peace Movements" in Lund, Sweden in August 1987 in co-operation with Lund University Peace Research Institute. The last meeting was organized as one of the working sessions of IPRA's conference in Rio de Janeiro in 1988.

Purpose
The object of the group is to promote a dialogue of peace researchers, historians, sociologists, and political scientists and others who are producing new works on the global peace movements. It seeks an exchange of ideas between East and West, North and South.

Publications
A book from the Lund conference, *Towards a Comparative Analysis of Peace Movements*, edited by Unto Vesa and Katsuya Kodama was published by Dartmouth Publishing Company in December 1989. You may follow the work of the group in IPRA Newsletter.

Contacts
Secretary-General of IPRA
Elise Boulding IPRA, Box 327, University of Colorado, Boulder, CO 80309-0327 U.S.A.

IPRA Study Group on Peace Movements
Nigel Young, Peace Studies, Colgate University, Hamilton, NY13346, U.S.A.
Katsuya Kodama (LUPRI), Finngatan 16, 223 62 Lund, Sweden